UNDISPUTED
NATIONAL

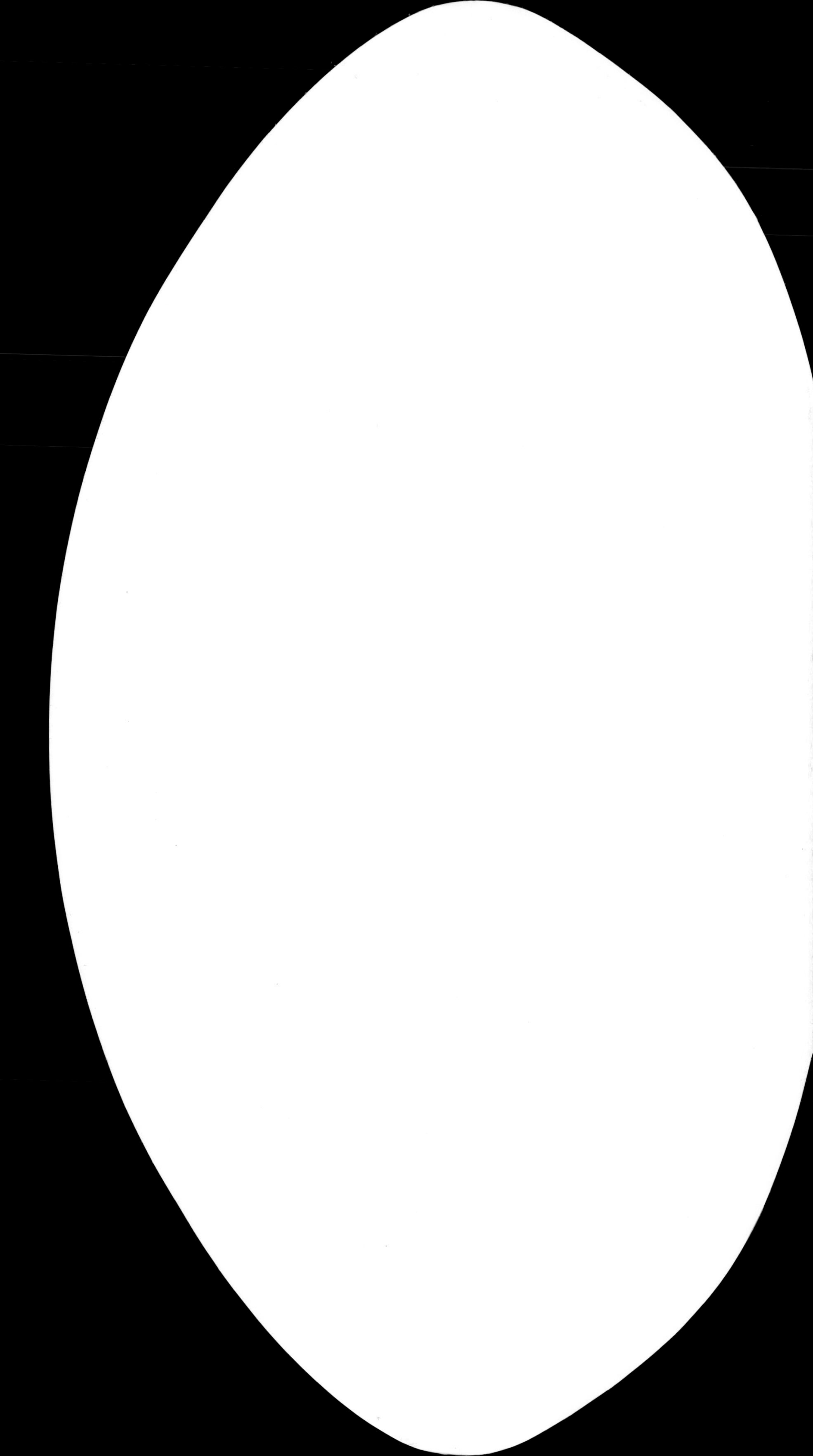

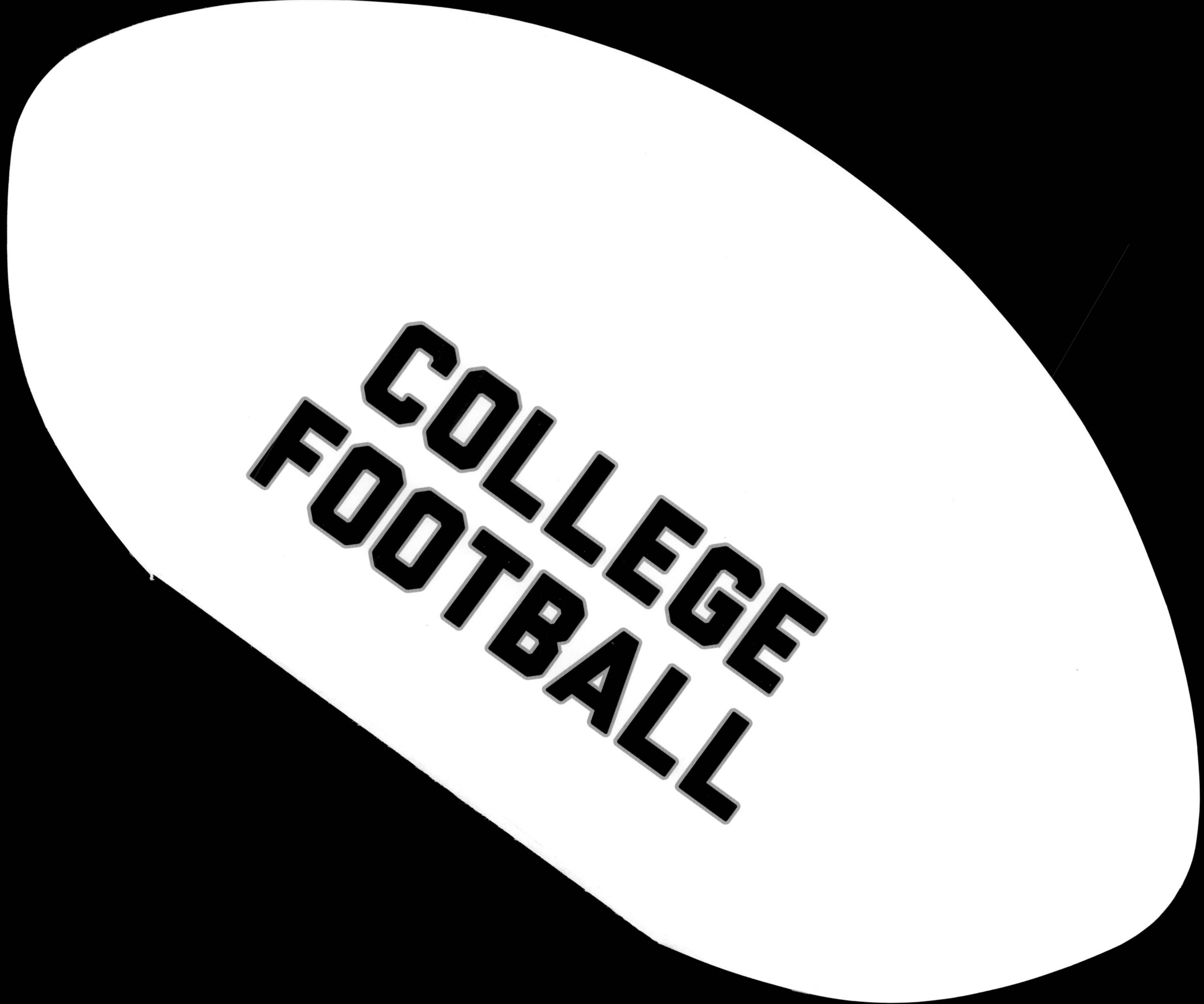
COLLEGE
FOOTBALL

ISBN 978-0-545-87759-6

Scholastic Inc., New York, NY
Printed in Beijing, China

This edition published by Scholastic Inc., 557 Broadway, New York, NY 10012 by arrangement with Ruckus Books. Scholastic and associated logos are trademarks and/or registered trademarks of Scholastic Inc.

Design: Compass Creative Studio Inc.
Author: Christopher Kubala

All Images: Getty Images
Editor: Faeryn Genovese

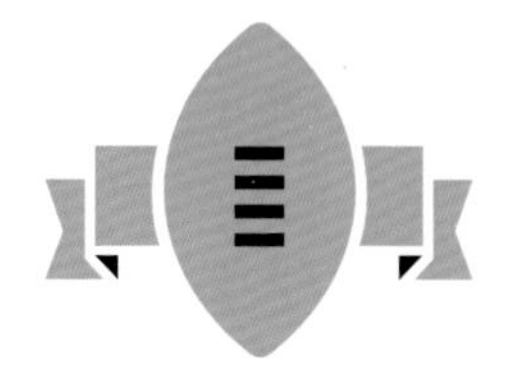

CONTENTS

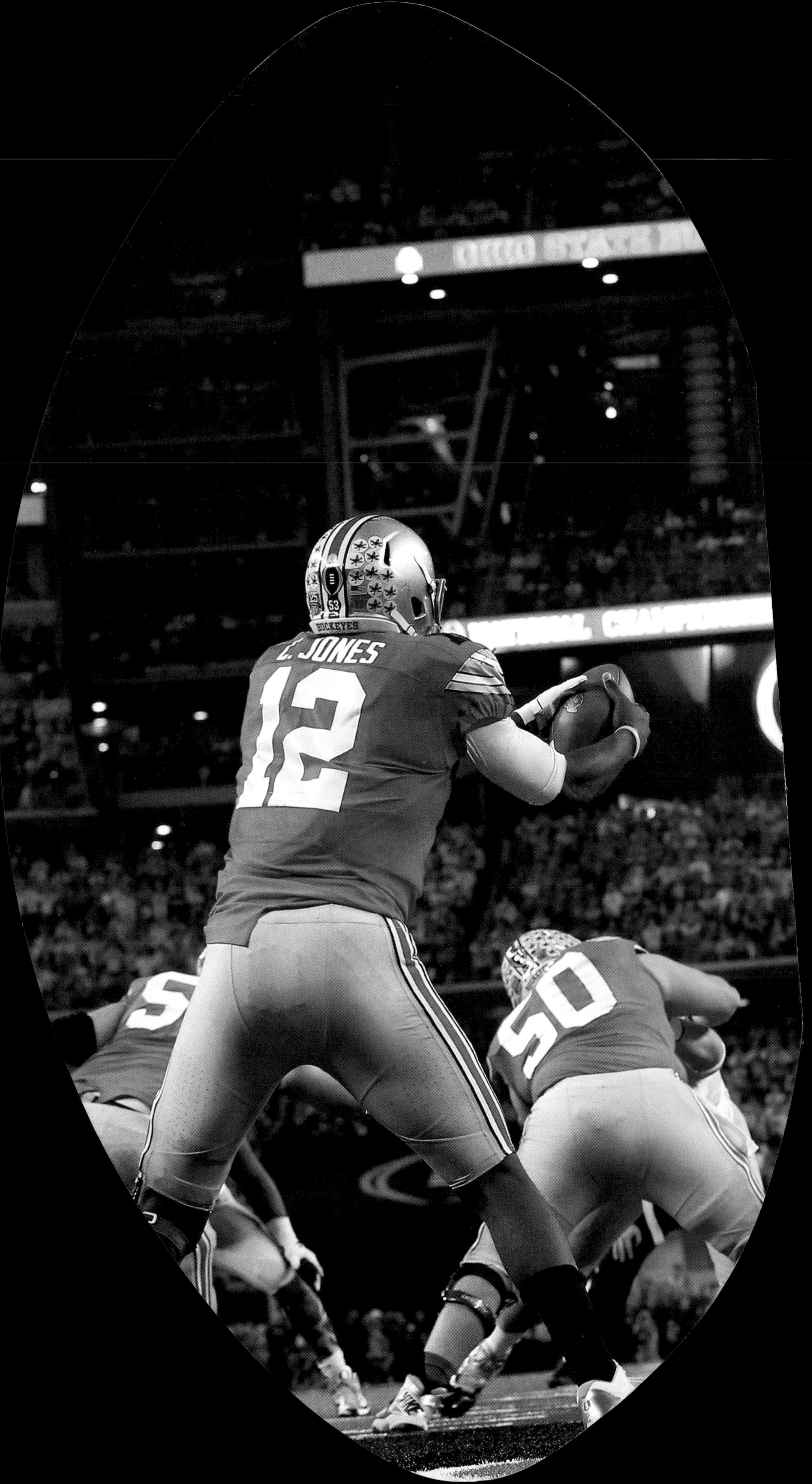
BUCKEYES
C. JONES
12
50

MEASUREMENT CONVERSIONS

IMPERIAL	METRIC
1 inch (in)	2.54 centimetres (cm)
1 foot (ft)	0.3048 metres (m)
1 yard (yd)	0.9144 metres (m)
1 mile (mi)	1.60934 kilometres (km)

DIMENSIONS OF A REGULATION COLLEGE FOOTBALL FIELD

	IMPERIAL	METRIC
LENGTH	360 feet (ft)	109.728 metres (m)
WIDTH	160 feet (ft)	48.768 metres (m)

2015
99

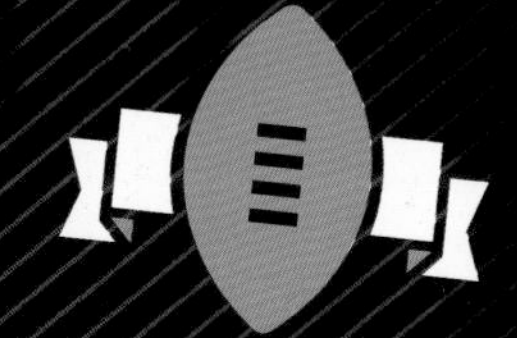

HISTORY OF

COLLEGE FOOTBALL

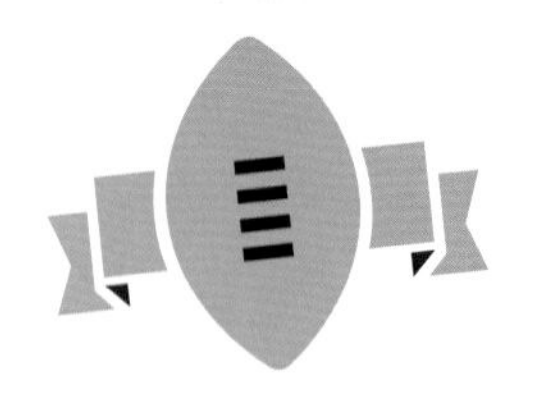

COLLEGE FOOTBALL

College football has evolved leaps and bounds since the first game was played over 140 years ago. Over that time, pioneers of the game have helped change the sport from a variant of soccer or rugby into the game that millions of fans enthusiastically watch on a weekly basis from late August into early January. College football can generate nearly half the revenue that a school's athletic department makes in a year.

The first intercollegiate football game took place on November 6, 1869, between Rutgers and Princeton. However, this contest was not anything close to what we identify with college football today, as it was played under the rules of association soccer that were written in 1863. In that contest, the field was 120 yards long and 75 yards wide and teams played with a round ball similar to a soccer ball. There were 25 players on a side, no officials, and teams scored by kicking the ball into the opposing team's net.

The way the rules worked was that any time a team scored, they were awarded one point, which was called a "game." Ten such games, meaning ten scores, was the limit of the contest, at which point a winning side would be determined. Rutgers was victorious over Princeton, then known as the College of New Jersey, by a count of 6-4. The two sides would meet a week later on Princeton's home field and, under slightly altered rules, Princeton was victorious in a lopsided 8-0 victory to even the series. The two sides were to originally have played three games against one another, but the third game was delayed because professors from both schools claimed that the games were interfering with the athletes' studies.

On October 20, 1873, four schools met at the Fifth Avenue Hotel in New York City to agree to rules and regulations to play a version of association soccer similar to the 1869 clash between Rutgers and Princeton. Indeed,

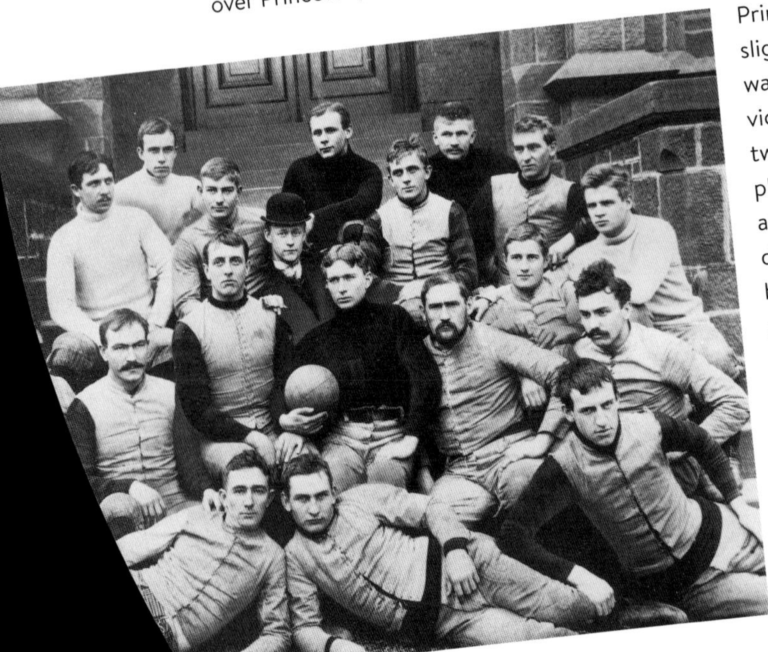

A group portrait of the Rutgers College football team, New Brunswick, NJ, 1891.

those two schools were among the four who were at the meeting, along with Yale and Columbia. Harvard was invited but declined, as they were interested in playing a more rough-and-tumble version of the sport, which at the time was known as "the Boston game."

"The Boston game" was still played with a round ball, but it incorporated other features that were not implemented in the rules of association soccer. Players could run with the ball, pass it, or dribble it instead of solely being limited to kicking it with their feet. Whoever had the ball was fair game to be tackled, though there were rules in place for dealing with over-the-top attempts at rough play. There was no limitation implemented as to the number of players a team could have on their side, but for the most part, it was limited to between 10 and 15.

Harvard had its first test of its new rules when they accepted a challenge from McGill University's rugby team. McGill is a school in Montreal, Quebec, Canada, and the sides agreed to play a pair of games. One game would be based on Harvard's rules and the other on the more stringent rules of rugby that McGill was familiar with. The games took place on the baseball field at Harvard's campus, known as Jarvis Field, on May 14 and 15, 1874. Harvard was victorious in the contest played under their rules and held their own against McGill under the rugby rules, playing to a scoreless draw. Harvard adopted some of the rugby rules to their own concept and thrived under them. In fall 1874, they made a trip to Montreal to play McGill on their home field and were victorious by a score of 3-0.

A portrait of two football players, United States, 1885.

THE BEGINNING OF COLLEGE FOOTBALL AS IT'S KNOWN TODAY

The first real steps toward the evolution of early college football into the game that is known and loved today were taken on June 4, 1875, when Harvard faced Tufts University in a game once again held at Jarvis Field on the Crimson campus. Tufts was victorious by a score of 1-0, but what made the game stand out was the differentiation of the rules from previous adaptations.

The first fundamental cornerstones of football were showcased in this contest: teams played 11 men to a side; the ball was no longer round but more egg shaped, like the football of today; and players were allowed to pick up the ball and run with it, with the play stopping when the player with the ball was knocked down or tackled. The College Football Hall of Fame has a picture of the victorious Tufts University team in its collection and recognizes the contest as the first official football game between two United States colleges.

The first conference for college football, the Intercollegiate Football Association (IFA), was founded in 1876. The meeting was held at the Massasoit House in Springfield, Massachusetts, which coincidentally would become the birthplace of basketball 15 years later. The original IFA consisted of Harvard, Princeton, and Columbia. Yale was present at the meeting but refused to join at the time due to a disagreement over the number of players allowed per team; they would eventually join in 1879. Meanwhile, Rutgers, the other school involved in the 1869 clash with Princeton, was not invited to the meeting at all. Most of the rules that were agreed upon at the time were basically straight out of the rugby rulebook, with one major exception. The schools agreed that points should be awarded for the actual scoring play itself (now known as a touchdown, but called a try in rugby), rather than just the conversion kick afterwards.

A crossbar that was 10 feet off the ground was implemented in 1876, altering

Football fans attending the Harvard vs Yale game at Harvard Stadium in Allston, Boston, MA, 1905.

the kicking game substantially, and the field was also shrunk down to nearly mirror today's dimensions. Still, the game was in its infancy and needed alterations and direction to take it to the next level of popularity. These early alterations to the sport and the rulebook would be made by Walter Camp, one of the first major pioneers of college football.

WALTER CAMP: FOOTBALL'S FIRST PIONEER

Walter Camp played football, or at least football in its earliest form, while attending Yale. Camp played the sport from 1876 to 1882 at the university and is considered the father of American football for his work in shaping the sport into what it is today. Camp overhauled the rules and added new concepts when he implemented his revisions, beginning in 1880.

The 1880 rules cut down the number of players on the field per side during any play in the game from 15 to 11. Camp also came up with the idea of having a play run from the line of scrimmage; in other words, the place where the previous play had ended. Instead of having a rugby-style scrum to determine possession, the team that had the ball would keep it, provided they could gain enough yardage to maintain possession. Thanks to this concept, Camp pioneered the snap from center.

In 1882 Camp made more important changes to football, making it more like the sport we know today. Camp instituted the down system, where teams had three downs to move the ball 5 yards. If they were unable to gain 5 yards in the three plays, the other team took possession of the ball at the spot where the last play concluded. This led to yard markers being painted on the field and the coining of the term "gridiron." The current system of four downs and 10 yards to gain a first down was not implemented

American football coach and executive Walter Chauncey Camp (1859-1925), known as the "father of American football," 1910s.

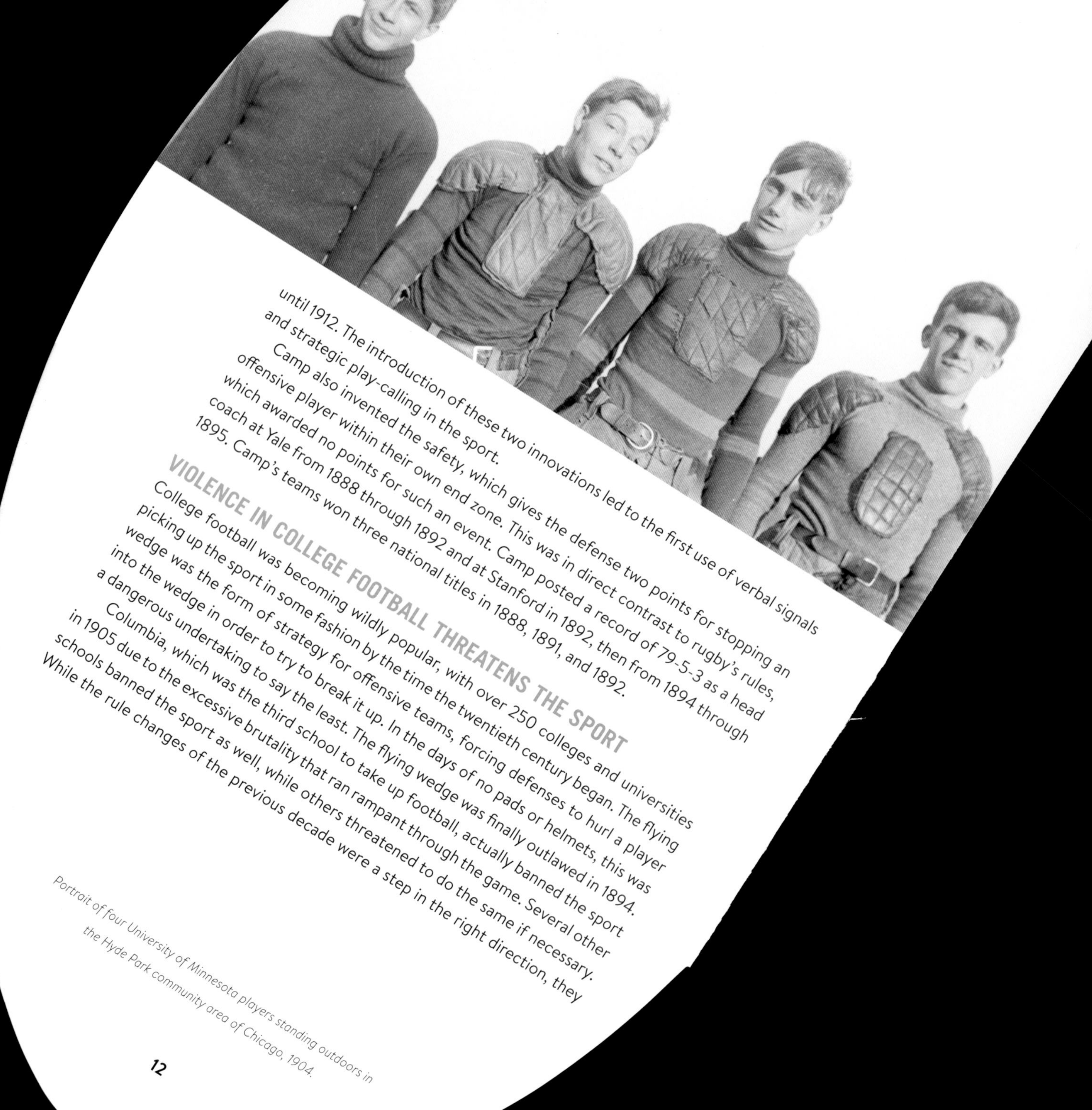

until 1912. The introduction of these two innovations led to the first use of verbal signals and strategic play-calling in the sport.

Camp also invented the safety, which gives the defense two points for stopping an offensive player within their own end zone. This was in direct contrast to rugby's rules, which awarded no points for such an event. Camp posted a record of 79-5-3 as a head coach at Yale from 1888 through 1892 and at Stanford in 1892, then from 1894 through 1895. Camp's teams won three national titles in 1888, 1891, and 1892.

VIOLENCE IN COLLEGE FOOTBALL THREATENS THE SPORT

College football was becoming wildly popular, with over 250 colleges and universities picking up the sport in some fashion by the time the twentieth century began. The flying wedge was the form of strategy for offensive teams, forcing defenses to hurl a player into the wedge in order to try to break it up. In the days of no pads or helmets, this was a dangerous undertaking to say the least. The flying wedge was finally outlawed in 1894.

Columbia, which was the third school to take up football, actually banned the sport in 1905 due to the excessive brutality that ran rampant through the game. Several other schools banned the sport as well, while others threatened to do the same if necessary. While the rule changes of the previous decade were a step in the right direction, they

Portrait of four University of Minnesota players standing outdoors in the Hyde Park community area of Chicago, 1904.

did not lead to a major decline in the number of serious injuries or deaths that resulted from on-the-field action.

The 1905 season saw an unprecedented and staggering 25 deaths, which prompted intervention. President Theodore Roosevelt, who was no lightweight himself, interjected himself into the fray. Roosevelt threatened to ban the sport completely, but settled for the implementation of a committee to revise the sport and make it safer and less violent. The situation would eventually lead to the formation and evolution of the National Collegiate Athletic Association (NCAA) in 1910.

Since its creation more than a century ago, the NCAA has been the driving force behind the rule changes and procedures that form the guidelines for its colleges and universities to follow regarding their athletic programs. Among these rule changes were those that allowed the forward pass, altered the equipment to help cut down on the number of injuries, and helped curb rough play.

OFFENSIVE EVOLUTION: THE FORWARD PASS MAKES ITS IMPACT

The first few decades of college football were rather one-dimensional. The running game was the basis of all offenses, as it was illegal to throw the ball forward from the line of scrimmage. This all changed in the early part of the twentieth century when a rule instituted in 1906 legalized the forward pass and added an entirely new dimension to the sport.

The first legal forward pass was thrown by Bradbury Robinson on September 6, 1906, for St. Louis University. The Billikens were coached by Eddie Cochems, who was the mastermind of one of the first sophisticated passing attacks in the history of the sport. The forward pass was slow to make an impact in the early stages of the sport, as it was not until rule changes in 1910 and 1912 that the horizons of the passing attack expanded.

West Virginia Wesleyan College, a small
l that had had no success against the
r West Virginia University in six
s, upset the Mountaineers

nceton, NJ,

route to an undefeated season. Future Hall quarterback and coach Earl “Greasy” Neale hauled three scores in that game. Prior to the 1912 upset, West Virginia Wesleyan had been no closer than a 36-0 drubbing in any of the six previous tilts between the schools.

Notre Dame also unveiled a heavy passing attack in 1913. The Irish, who were a decent football program at the time, went in and walloped Army, 35-13. Knute Rockne, future Notre Dame coach and College Football Hall of Fame inductee, caught a touchdown pass in that contest. The shellacking was the only defeat Army would take during the season. Additional rule changes in the 1920s, including an alteration to the size and shape of the ball, would further enhance passing attacks, which became far more commonplace in the 1930s.

CHANGES IN THE SCORING SYSTEM

When football was played under its original set of rules, teams were awarded one point for scoring, which resulted in low scores like 1-0 that are no longer seen in football today. The initial changes in the scoring system came in 1883, and in sticking with the soccer and rugby ties to the sport, scoring via the kicking game was more valuable than other manners. Field goals were worth five points and touchdowns, along with their subsequent conversions, were worth four points apiece.

The next year, 1884, saw the increase of points awarded for a safety from one point to two. That scoring change has remained in effect ever since. Another change in scoring came in 1897 as touchdowns were increased from four points to five, while conversions after touchdowns were reduced to the current one point that they have been ever since. Field goals were reduced from five points to four in 1904 and then to the three points they are worth today in 1909. Touchdowns were raised from five to the current six-point value in 1912.

John Heisman, head coach of the Georgia Tech Yellow Jackets, poses for a photo circa 1904-1919. Heisman coached the Yellow Jackets from 1904-1919 and

The scoring system would remain constant for the next 40-plus years, with the next change coming in 1958. This was the advent of the two-point conversion: teams now had the option of either kicking the ball for the extra point after a touchdown, or trying to score from the 3-yard line via the run or the pass. If successful, the team would be awarded two points. The line of scrimmage was moved from the 2 to the 3-yard line for conversions at this point.

In 1988 a further change was implemented that awarded the defensive team two points if they were able to return a blocked extra-point attempt or interception across the opposing goal line. This was amended again in 1992 to include any fumble that occurred outside the end zone being returned the distance on a conversion attempt. The NCAA also made the decision to eliminate tie games and institute overtime beginning in the 1996 regular season, though the system was in place for the 1995 bowl season. The 1995 Las Vegas Bowl between Toledo and Nevada was the first college football game to go into overtime. Toledo was victorious by a score of 40-37.

MAJOR CONTRIBUTORS TO COLLEGE FOOTBALL

John Heisman was a major player in the furtherance of college football. He was the head coach at Georgia Tech from 1904 to 1919. The school never had a losing record in his 16 seasons at the helm and Heisman left the school with a .779 winning percentage (102-29-7), the best mark in school history. Georgia Tech also won the first of its four national titles under Heisman in 1917 and boasted a 33-game winning streak. The school was 37-4-2 in his final five years at the school.

Heisman is also known for being the head coach of the Georgia Tech program when it was part of the most one-sided game in college football history. Georgia Tech crushed Cumberland by a score of 222-0 in 1916, a game that has lived on for nearly a century as the worst beating in sports. During his coaching career, which began in 1892 and ended in 1926, Heisman coached at Oberlin College, Buchtel College (now the University of Akron), the Agricultural and Mechanical College of Alabama (now Auburn), Clemson, Penn, Washington & Jefferson, and finally at Rice.

Heisman was at the forefront of the movement to legalize the forward pass. This was in direct contrast to Walter Camp, who wasn't a fan of the innovation. Heisman also came up with the center snap to start the play, and his Heisman—or "jump shift"—formation was the predecessor to the more modern T and I formations that were common in later years. The I-formation is still extremely common in the current era, while the T-formation is not used as much as it was back in the 1930s and 1940s. Heisman is additionally known for the development of shoulder and hip pads, helping

...ty over the late nineteenth century, and he ...th the invention of the scoreboard and dividing ...e into quarters.

After Heisman's coaching days were finished, he was named the director of athletics at the Downtown Athletic Club in New York City. While he was working in the position, the concept of the Downtown Athletic Club Award, to be given to college football's top player, was conceived. The first time it was awarded was in 1935, to running back Jay Berwanger of the University of Chicago. Heisman died on October 3, 1936, at the age of 66. Shortly thereafter, the Downtown Athletic Club chose to rename its award the Heisman Trophy to honor Heisman's contributions to the game. To this day the trophy still bears his name.

Another major pioneer in the history of college football was Amos Alonzo Stagg. Stagg played for Yale before coaching and was named to the first All-American team in 1889. He began coaching in 1890 at the Springfield, Massachusetts, YMCA, which is now known as Springfield College. It was the start of an illustrious coaching career that spanned parts of seven decades. Among the players on Stagg's roster was the future Dr. James Naismith, who would later invent basketball at the school. Stagg would score the only basket for the Springfield College faculty in the first public exhibition of Naismith's basketball, a 5-1 victory for the students of the school.

Stagg coached the University of Chicago football team from 1892 to 1932, was the head coach at Pacific from 1932 through 1946, and then was an assistant at Susquehanna under his son through 1952 before finally retiring in an official capacity. He would go on to be an unpaid advisory coach at Stockton Junior College until he retired from that in 1960, at the age of 98. Stagg was the first person inducted into the College Football Hall of Fame as both a player and a coach.

Stagg amassed a record of 314-199-35 in his head coaching career. He spent 41 seasons as the head coach at the University of Chicago, posting a record of 242 victories against just 112

Chicago back Jay Berwanger (1933-35), 1935 Consensus All-America selection and first winner of the Heisman Trophy, gained 4,108 yards in the three years he played.

defeats and 27 ties. Stagg helped lead the school to seve
Ten Conference championships in his time at the school. The
school was one of the biggest powerhouses in college football
for the first quarter of the twentieth century. In addition to his
work in football, Stagg also coached the basketball team for
one season, the track team for 32 seasons, and the baseball
team for 19. He is credited with inventing the batting cage.

In football, Stagg's contributions are noteworthy and
impressive. He helped organize the Big Ten Conference, which
at the time was known as the Western Conference, and was a
founder of the American Football Coaches Association. Stagg
is also widely recognized for the invention of the tackling
dummy and the innovation of teams huddling between plays,
and he has also been credited with the concept of awarding
varsity letters and the addition of uniform numbers to help
identify players. On the field, Stagg is credited with the lateral,
along with plays like the reverse and putting a man in motion.
The fake punt and quick kick have also been attributed to him.
Stagg served on the first rules committee that the NCAA
instituted and was at the forefront of helping the game's
continued evolution. Stagg advocated for padded goalposts
to prevent players from sustaining serious injury from running
into them, and in 1927 the goalposts were moved from the
front of the end zone back 10 yards to the back line of the end
zone, further reducing the potential for injuries taking place.
He is well known for his work as a strategist, devising different
plays and formations. As legendary Notre Dame coach Knute
Rockne once said: "All football comes from Stagg."

Considering Stagg's accomplishments of 12 league
championships, two national titles, and 314 victories, it is hard
to rebut Rockne's statement. The championship game for
Division III schools is known as the Amos Alonzo Stagg Bowl, a
tribute to his achievements on and off the field. Stagg died in
1965 in his sleep at the age of 102.

Glenn "Pop" Warner is synonymous with college football,
with football for younger children with the Pop Warner

...els with a football on his knee.
...y of Chicago and was

league. Warner played his college football at Cornell from 1892 through 1894 then took to the coaching ranks, where he would string together a career that would last more than 40 years. Warner coached in college football from 1896 through the 1938 season as a head coach before finishing his career with a one-year stint as an associate coach at San Jose State in 1939.

Warner coached during two different periods at his alma mater of Cornell, along with a pair of stints at Carlisle Indian. He also coached at Iowa State, Pittsburgh, Stanford, and Temple, while beginning his coaching career with Georgia. On three separate occasions, Warner was coaching two teams simultaneously. He coached Georgia and Iowa State in 1895 and 1896, Iowa State and Cornell in 1897 and 1898, and Iowa State along with Carlisle Indian in 1899.

Warner would win four national titles in his coaching career: three at Pittsburgh in a span of four years and one with Stanford. Warner won national championships at Pittsburgh in 1915, 1916, and 1918, then claimed his fourth with the Cardinal in 1926. While at Carlisle for his second time as the head coach, Warner had the legendary Jim Thorpe on his team roster. Warner had a record of 319 victories, 106 defeats, and 32 ties when he officially retired from coaching. Those figures do not include the 18-8 record he posted as the co-coach of Iowa State.

Warner brought several innovations to college football during his tenure. He came up with the idea of the single and double wing formations, and was the mind behind one of the more popular plays in football today, the screen pass. Warner also was behind the implementation of shoulder and thigh pads to help protect players from injuries. He devised the idea of having white helmets for ends and red helmets for running backs and the quarterback, helping to differentiate between players. Warner was inducted into the College Football Hall of Fame in 1951. He died of throat cancer on September 7, 1954, at the age of 83.

Head coach Glenn Scobey "Pop" Warner of the Stanford Cardinal gets ready for a practice circa 1932 in Palo Alto, CA. Warner

HISTORY OF NATIONAL CHAMPIONS

For as long as there has been football, there has been clamoring for naming a champion to determine who the best of the best is in the sport. In the early days, there were a slew of different polls and individuals who made their choice for a national champion. This has been more streamlined in recent years, with the two major remaining national champion polls being the Associated Press, which represents the media's votes, and the UPI, which is voted on by college football coaches. The coaches' poll was the brainchild of Leo Petersen and has been in use since 1950.

Since the inception of the bowl era and the first declaration of a national champion by the Associated Press in 1936, Alabama has claimed the most national championships with a total of 10. By virtue of their win over Oregon in the College Football Playoff national championship game, Ohio State is tied for second-most with eight; Notre Dame has eight as well, though their last title came back in 1988. USC and Oklahoma each have seven national titles in that span, and Miami (FL) and Nebraska are the only other schools that have claimed as many as five national championships since 1936.

When it comes to the history of the national championship, it is interesting to note that no school outside the Ivy League won a national title prior to the year 1900. Michigan was the first school outside the Ivy League constituents to claim a national championship, winning the title in both 1901 and 1902. The Wolverines were also co-champions in 1903 and 1904, sharing the title with Princeton in 1903 and Penn in 1904. In that four-year span, the Wolverines were as dominant as any team has been in the sport, going 43-0-1 in 44 games and outscoring their opponents by an astounding 2,292 points (2,326 to 34). A 6-6 tie against Minnesota on October 31, 1903, was the only blemish in that span under Fielding Yost.

A more in-depth look at the numbers Michigan put up during that time shows just how complete the Wolverines' ...mination over their opponents was. ... went the entire 1901 season

...lley carries the football and scores ... ...mber 29, 1946, at Griffith

without allowing a point on the board, outscoring opponents by a count of 550-0. Included in that was a 128-0 rout of Buffalo and an 89-0 whipping of Beloit. The Wolverines gave up a dozen points in 1901, and wiped out Michigan State 119-0, blanked Iowa 107-0, and drubbed Ohio State 86-0. The six points Minnesota scored in the tie on Halloween in 1903 were the only points the Wolverines allowed all season. Michigan would blast Kalamazoo 95-0 and West Virginia by the blowout margin of 130-0 in 1904. A 2-0 defeat at the hands of Amos Alonzo Stagg's Chicago team in the 1905 season finale ended the Wolverines' unbeaten string at 56 games and marked the first loss in Yost's coaching career at the school.

Yost would amass a record of 165-29-10 while at Michigan, coaching there from 1901 through 1923, then again in the 1925 and 1926 campaigns. The Wolverines claimed six national championships during his reign. Yost was also responsible, along with Michigan athletic director Charles Baird, for creating college football's first bowl game, the Rose Bowl. Michigan played in the inaugural Rose Bowl on New Year's Day 1902, walloping Stanford, one of Yost's former employers, by a score of 49-0.

The Associated Press originally declared their national champion prior to bowl games being completed. They changed that method for the 1965 season and dropped it in favor of the regular season for 1966 and 1967, only to then go back to declaring their national champion after the conclusion of bowl games in the 1968 season. Meanwhile, the coaches' poll went to determining their national champion after bowl games in the 1974 season. Teams that are on probation by the NCAA are ineligible for consideration in the coaches' poll, while the Associated Press poll still allows for their inclusion. The Football Writers Association of America (FWAA) has selected a national champion since 1954; they make their choice after the bowl games.

Minnesota won three of the first six AP national championships, but they only have

Halfback Tom Harmon (#98) of the Michigan Wolverines poses for a portrait circa 1940. He was the 1940 Heisman Trophy winner.

claimed one since 1941, when they were named the AP, UPI, and NFF champions in 1960. Mississippi got the nod from the FWAA that year. There have been several split national champions in the history of the sport, the first coming in 1954, when the AP national champion was Ohio State, while the coaches went with UCLA. Split national champions also occurred in 1957 (Auburn for the AP, Ohio State UPI), 1965 (Alabama was the AP national champ, Michigan State the UPI), 1970 (Nebraska AP, Texas UPI), 1973 (Notre Dame AP, Alabama UPI), 1974 (Oklahoma AP, USC UPI) and 1978 (Alabama AP, USC UPI).

There would be 11 years of harmonious agreement between the two polls before the next disagreement in 1990. That year saw Colorado claim the AP crown, while Georgia Tech took the UPI national championship. The same issue recurred the next year, as Miami (FL) was the AP national champion, while Washington claimed the coaches' poll. The 1997 season also had split national champions, as Michigan claimed the AP championship and Nebraska was the coaches' poll selection. The 1973 split national championship was particularly galling, as Alabama lost the Sugar Bowl to Notre Dame 24-23, but the Crimson Tide had already been named the UPI national champion before the bowl games. The next season, the decision was made to render the UPI champion following bowl games.

In 1998 college football adopted the BCS, or Bowl Championship Series system. Under that format, the #1 and #2 ranked teams in the country at the end of the regular season and conference championship games faced each other for the right to be named national champion. This has produced a split national champion only once since its inception, when in 2003 #3 in the AP poll, Oklahoma, was selected to play in the national championship game against

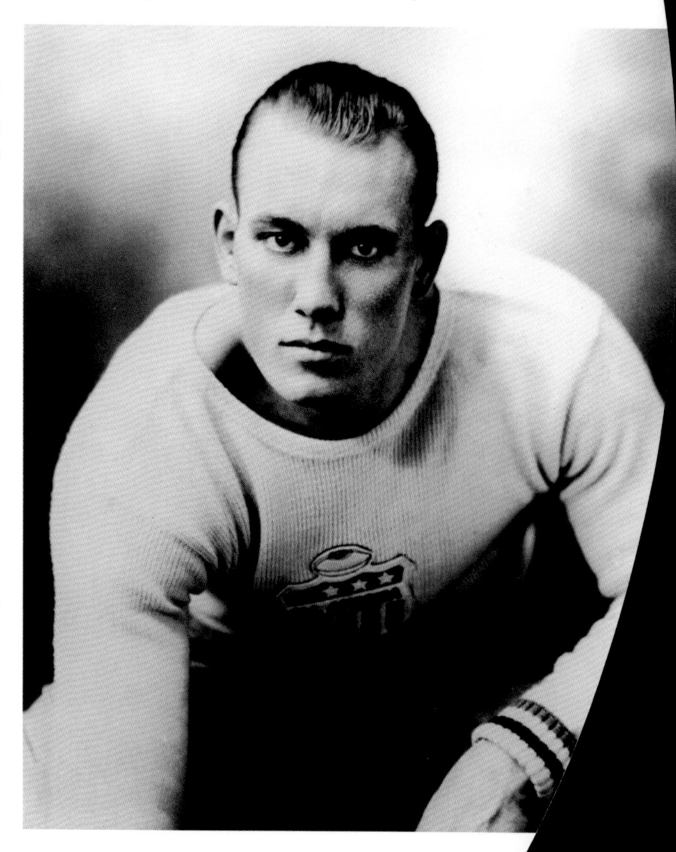

Portrait of Frank "Bruiser" Kinard (1914-1985), tackle for the University of Mississippi, in his All-America jersey, 1937.

#2 LSU, leaving #1 USC out of the mix. LSU would go on to defeat Oklahoma 21-14 to claim the BCS national championship and USC claimed the AP and FWAA crowns.

In the BCS era, the Southeastern Conference dominated the landscape, claiming eight of the 14 BCS championships. Alabama, Florida, and LSU have won two national crowns apiece, while Auburn and Tennessee each have one. Oklahoma and Texas both have wins to represent the Big 12 Conference, while no other conference has more than one national championship to their credit. The Big East claimed a championship in 2001 when Miami won, though the team defected to the ACC in 2004. Additionally, the Big Ten (Ohio State in 2002) and the ACC (Florida State in 2000) Conferences have each won a BCS championship. USC won a national title for the Pac-12 Conference in 2004, but it was vacated after violations involving improper benefits were found to have taken place.

MAJOR COACHING FIGURES IN COLLEGE FOOTBALL

There have been 12 coaches as of the conclusion of the 2014 season who have won at least 300 games in the history of college football. Ten of the twelve who have broken the 300-win plateau have been inducted into the College Football Hall of Fame. The exceptions to that group are Larry Kehres and Ken Sparks. Kehres compiled 317 victories in his 26 seasons at Mount Union, a Division III powerhouse, and has a phenomenal .926 winning percentage, having gone 317-24-3 since 1986. Along the way, Mount Union won 10 Division III national championships since 1993 and posted a win streak of 110 regular season games that spanned 1994 through 2005. Ken Sparks from Carson-Newman joined the 300-game club in the 2012 season and is still coaching for the school.

The all-time leader in victories in college football's coaching pantheon is John Gagliardi. Gagliardi coached at St. John's (MN) from 1953 until 2012, after spending 1949 through 1952 at Carroll College in Montana. In his coaching career, Gagliardi put together a record of 489 victories, 138 defeats, and 11 ties for a .775 winning percentage. Under his guidance, St. John's (MN) claimed four national championships, most recently in 2003.

The all-time leader in victories on the Division I level of college football is former Penn State coach Joe Paterno. Paterno won 409 games, while losing 136 and tying three games in his career with the Nittany Lions. He coached at the school 46 years before being ousted in November 2011 in the wake of the Jerry Sandusky indictment. Paterno led the Nittany Lions to two national championships in 1982 and 1986, along with three Big Ten Conference titles. A 10-7 victory over Illinois on October 29, 2011, gave Paterno his 409th career victory, the most among all Division I coaches, breaking the mark set by Eddie Robinson.

Paterno also holds college football records for bowl game victories with 24, and appearances with 37. He posted a mark of 24-12-1 in bowl games and is the only coach who won each of the four major bowl games (the Rose, Sugar, Fiesta, and Orange) at least once. He additionally won the Cotton Bowl Classic, which was a major bowl at one point in the history of college football. Penn State had five unbeaten, untied seasons under Paterno's guidance, though in four of those seasons, the Nittany Lions did not win a national title. Paterno died on January 22, 2012, at the age of 85.

The previous record holder for Division I victories was Eddie Robinson of Grambling, who won 408 games over the course of his career. Robinson coached Grambling in 1941 and 1942, and then from 1945 through the 1997 season. Robinson retired with a career mark of 408 victories, 165 losses, and 15 ties, which was good for a .707 winning percentage. Robinson isn't as commonplace a name as some of the others on the list due to coaching a school that was a historically black college or university. Grambling turned out over 100 NFL players during Robinson's tenure, including Pro Football Hall of Famers Willie Brown, Buck Buchanan, Charlie Joiner, and Willie Davis. The school won 17 Southwestern Athletic Conference titles and nine black college football national championships under Robinson.

Bobby Bowden of Florida State fame is fourth on the all-time victories list for

Joe Paterno of Penn State University looks on, circa 1970s.

...n. Bowden was on the winning side 377 times in his career, ...a four ties. Bowden also coached at Samford and West Virginia ...Florida State in 1976. He stayed at Florida State through the 2009 ...il he was replaced by Jimbo Fisher. Bowden was forced to vacate 12 wins ...he 2006 and 2007 seasons for games that featured an ineligible player, which reduced his title from the 389 that he previously had. The Seminoles won a pair of national titles and a dozen ACC championships under him. He also led Florida State to a 14-season stretch between 1987 and 2000 where the Seminoles won at least 10 games and finished in the top five of the AP poll.

Perhaps one of the best known coaches of all time is Alabama's Paul "Bear" Bryant. Bryant was an institution in Tuscaloosa, coaching the Crimson Tide from 1958 through 1982. Bryant is so entwined with the history of the Crimson Tide that it is easy to overlook that he also coached at Maryland (1945), Kentucky (1946-1953), and Texas A&M (1954-1957) before ever setting foot on the Alabama campus. Once there, Bryant was as well known for his houndstooth or gingham hats as he was for winning football games.

While Bryant was at Alabama, the Crimson Tide won six national championships and 13 SEC championship crowns. Alabama won back-to-back national championships twice under Bryant in 1964-65 and then again in 1978-79. All told, Bryant had a record of 232-46-9 at Alabama, and finished with an overall coaching mark of 323 wins, 85 defeats, and 17 ties. He was the winningest coach in college football history when he retired in 1982; he stands sixth now.

Until Nick Saban took over the job at Alabama, the school had been through tumultuous times. From Bryant's retirement in 1982 through Saban's hiring in time for the 2007 campaign, Alabama went through six coaches (seven if Mike Price is factored

Grambling University head football coach Eddie Robinson speaks with players on the sidelines during a game against Hampton at Giants Stadium in East Rutherford, N.J.

in, though he was removed following a scandal before he ever coached a game at the school). Alabama's national championship win in 2012 under Saban was the school's first since Gene Stallings delivered a championship in 1992.

MARQUEE PROGRAMS IN COLLEGE FOOTBALL

Almost every school has had their fifteen minutes of fame when it comes to college football: a stunning upset victory, a shining moment, a special season where everything seemed to fall just right. Then there are the perennial powers, teams that have been successful year in and year out, dominating long stretches of time at the top of their conference or the rankings. In the history of major college football, no school has amassed more than the 889 victories Michigan has to their credit. The Wolverines are one of six schools in the Football Bowl Subdivision to win at least 800 games, while a total of 15 have been victorious at least 700 times in the history of their programs. Michigan is followed in the top five by Alabama (864 wins), Nebraska (839 victories), Texas (830 wins), and Penn State, which has recorded 827 victories.

Notre Dame is the only other school with 800 wins as they have 805, though Oklahoma should join the group in 2015 as they currently have 797. An interesting note is that of the schools with at least 700 all-time wins through the 2015 season, 14 of them are still fielding active teams on the Division I-A or Football Bowl Subdivision level. Yale, which is 13th all-time with 718 wins, moved down to Division I-AA, or the Football Championship Subdivision, in 1982 rather than continuing to attempt to compete against the powerhouse schools in major conferences.

In the latter stages of the nineteenth century and

Head Coach Paul "Bear" Bryant of the Alabama Crimson Tide watches play from the sidelines during an NCAA football game against Rutgers University, October 11, 1980, at Giant Stadium in East Rutherford, NJ.

entieth century, the Ivy League schools were the dominant tball. In fact, from the sport's inception in 1869 until Michigan ional championship for the first time in 1901, every national championship ed by an Ivy League school. In the years spanning 1890 to 1900, the national mpionships were claimed by Yale four times, Harvard three times, Princeton twice, and Pennsylvania twice. For all their dominance in the early stages of college football, the Ivy League's last national champion came in 1922, when Princeton won the National Championship Foundation's title along with California.

The decade that spanned 1911 through 1920 started off with a distinct Ivy League feel, much like the first 30 years of the sport. Harvard took three championships in four years, winning in 1910, 1912, and 1913. Their run was interrupted solely by a 6-2-1 season in 1911 when Princeton claimed the national title. In that season, Harvard was defeated by Princeton and Carlisle Indian (with Jim Thorpe), while battling Yale to a scoreless tie. Army (1914), Cornell (1915), and Georgia Tech (1917) would all win their first national crowns in the decade. Pittsburgh won one national championship and claimed a share of two more (1910 shared with Harvard, outright champion in 1916, shared with Michigan in 1918). The 1919 season saw a three-way championship when Harvard, Texas A&M, and Notre Dame were all named champion by the National Championship Foundation. The decade ended with California claiming the 1920 national title as their first.

As college football continued to grow in popularity during the fledgling years of the National Football League, a smaller group of schools began crowding the top of the end-of-year rankings and claiming national championships. Both Alabama (1925, 1926) and Notre Dame (1929, 1930) won back-to-back national championships, and the Irish also added one in 1924 for good measure. Cornell won the national championship in 1921 and also was part of a split national championship with California and Princeton a year later. Illinois claimed a pair of national crowns, in 1923 with the legendary Red Grange and again in 1927, while Georgia Tech (1928), Michigan (split with Illinois in 1923), and Stanford (shared with Alabama in 1926) were also

The University of California, Los Angeles Bruins take on the University of Michigan Wolverines during a 1983 NCAA game at the

in the mix.

The 1930s were dominated by Big Ten Conference teams, w of the ten national championships in the decade. Minnesota, which wa dominant programs in the nation, claimed three of those four, winning back-to-back titles in 1934, 1935, and 1936. The 1936 championship was the first year that th Associated Press began declaring a national champion. Michigan won the other national championship for the conference in the decade in 1933. The University of Southern California won back-to-back championships in 1931 and 1932, Pittsburgh won their first national championship since 1918 in 1937, and Texas A&M claimed their first title since 1919 in 1939. Texas Christian University won their first national championship in 1938.

The 1940s saw just five schools win the ten national championships, with the Big Ten Conference claiming four of those crowns for the second consecutive decade. Minnesota took the first two titles of the 1940s in 1940 and 1941, giving them five national championships in an eight-year span. Ohio State would win a national championship in 1942, while Michigan would stake their claim for the school and the

Group portrait of Knute Rockne's famous backfield at Notre Dame, from left to right: quarterback Frank Carideo, fullback Joe Savoldi, halfback Marchmont Schwartz, and halfback Marty Brill, South Bend, ID, November 12, 1930.

Big Ten Conference in 1948. Army won back-to-back championships with Glenn Davis and Doc Blanchard running wild. "Mr. Outside" and "Mr. Inside" led Army to a period of dominance in the mid-1940s and national championships in 1944 and 1945. The rest of the 1940s belonged to the Notre Dame Fighting Irish. Notre Dame would win four national championships, in 1943 and then three in a four-year span, in 1946, 1948, and 1949. The Irish would also produce three Heisman Trophy winners as Angelo Bertelli (1943), John Lujack (1947), and Leon Hart (1949) would all be honored with the coveted award.

Bud Wilkinson and the Oklahoma Sooners were as dominant a team as could be found during the 1950s. The school went 93-10-3 in the decade, winning three national championships in 1950, 1955, and 1956. The Sooners were also undefeated in 1954 but finished third in the rankings, as UCLA won the FWAA and UPI national championships and Ohio State was named the AP champion. Oklahoma rung up a record 47-game win streak between 1953 and 1957 under Wilkinson, a record that has never been seriously threatened. Toledo has the next longest winning streak, a 35-game run from 1969 to 1971. Wilkinson also led Oklahoma to an NCAA record 74-game conference unbeaten streak that was snapped by Nebraska on October 31, 1959.

Ohio State claimed a pair of national championships in the 1950s, splitting with UCLA in 1954 and then winning the FWAA and UPI portions of the national title in 1957. Auburn claimed the AP title that year. Tennessee (1951), Michigan State (1952), Maryland (1953), Syracuse (1959), LSU, and Iowa (split national title in 1958, with LSU taking the UPI and AP championships while Iowa claimed the FWAA championship) all won their first national championship in school history. Syracuse was led by Ernie

Football player Harold "Red" Grange in his first year at the University of Illinois with his freshman football coach, Bert Ingwerson, Urbana, IL, 1922.

Davis, who was the first African American to claim the Heisman Trophy when he won the award in 1961.

The 1960s brought some of the usual suspects to the national championship party. Ohio State, Notre Dame, Alabama, and USC all claimed titles. Michigan State won split national championships in both 1965 and 1966. The 1966 split championship was with Notre Dame. The two schools battled to a 10-10 tie in East Lansing in November of that year in a game that was billed as the "Game of the Century" and was well noted for Ara Parseghian's cautious play-calling in the final minute with a chance to go for the win. The tie preserved both schools' undefeated marks and would prove wise, as Notre Dame crushed USC the next week and would claim the AP championship. Texas won national titles in 1963 and 1969, Ohio State in 1961 and 1968, Alabama in 1961, 1964, and 1965, and USC in 1962 and 1967.

The 1970s saw the major power conferences dominate the national championship landscape. Alabama (consensus champion in 1979, AP champ 1978, UPI champ 1973) and USC (consensus 1972, UPI in 1974 and 1978) both won three national championships. Additionally, Nebraska (1970 AP, FWAA, 1971 consensus), Notre Dame (1973 AP, FWAA, NFF, 1977 consensus), and Oklahoma (1974 AP, 1975 consensus) all staked claims to two national titles. Texas won the NFF and UPI titles for the second consecutive year in 1970, while Pittsburgh, led by running back Tony Dorsett, was the consensus national champion in 1976.

The 1980s brought a new college football power to the forefront. The Miami (FL) Hurricanes were dominant, winning three national titles and narrowly missing a fourth in 1986. That year, Penn State pulled an upset, defeating the Hurricanes 14-10 in the Fiesta Bowl, allowing the Nittany Lions

Syracuse's Ernie Davis (#44) in action, rushing for a 57-yard touchdown as Roger Davis (#69) blocks vs West Virginia, Syracuse, NY.

t in the polls to #1 and sending Miami from #1 to #2. Miami was g their second national title of the decade a year later in 1987 and third in 1989. The Hurricanes won their first national title in 1983, capped a thrilling 31-30 Orange Bowl victory over Nebraska. In that game, Nebraska coach Tom Osborne opted to go for a two-point conversion after scoring to pull within one point, only to have Miami safety Ken Calhoun knock away Turner Gill's pass. Penn State was the only other school to win multiple national titles in the 1980s, winning in 1982 and 1986. Georgia won in 1980 behind Herschel Walker, while Clemson (1981), BYU (1984), Oklahoma (1985), and Notre Dame (1988) claimed one each.

The 1990s started out with back-to-back split national champions in 1990 (Colorado and Georgia Tech) and 1991 (Miami (FL) and Washington). The decade was dominated by Nebraska (consensus championships in 1994 and 1995, and split champion in 1997 with Michigan) and Florida State (consensus championships in 1993 and 1999). Alabama (1992), Florida (1996), and Tennessee (1998) also laid claim to national titles. The 1998 season was the first year of the Bowl Championship Series, which pitted the top two teams in the country against each other in a de facto national championship contest. Tennessee prevailed over Florida State 23-16 to win the national title.

Since the advent of the BCS in 1998, there has been just one instance of a split national champion. That came in 2003, when the BCS championship, along with the coaches' poll, went to LSU, who beat Oklahoma in the Sugar Bowl. However, the AP had USC #1 in their poll going into the bowl games and when the Trojans beat Michigan 28-14 in the Rose Bowl, they remained in the top spot on the AP ballot and thus were crowned the AP champions. This was mainly due to Oklahoma, which was #1 most of the season, getting walloped by Kansas State 35-7 in the Big 12 Championship. Oklahoma remained #1

Albert Bentley (#16) of the Miami Hurricanes carries the ball during a game against the West Virginia Mountaineers in the Orange Bowl

in the BCS standings due to strength of schedule and rank. The 2003 season was hugely controversial, as USC, Oklahoma, and LSU all were one-loss teams going into the bowl season, as were mid-major teams Boise State, TCU, and Miami (OH).

Since 2000, the Southeastern Conference has been dominant, winning eight of the 14 national titles, with Alabama claiming three (2009, 2011, 2012), LSU (2003, 2007) and Florida (2006, 2008) each claiming a pair, and Auburn taking one in 2010. The SEC had won seven straight national championships from 2006 through 2012.

The SEC's string of dominance was snapped in 2013 as Auburn was unable to hold on to a 21-3 second quarter lead against Florida State. The Seminoles reeled off 17 unanswered points to cut the deficit to 21-20 early in the fourth. The Tigers kicked a field goal to extend their lead to 24-20 with 4:42 to play but gave up a 100-yard kick return for a score by Florida State's Levonte Whitfield, giving Florida State a 27-24 edge. Auburn rallied once again to take a 31-27 advantage with 1:19 to play on Tre Mason's 37-yard scoring run but the Tigers couldn't hold on.

Jameis Winston, who won the Heisman Trophy as a freshman at quarterback for the Seminoles, led Florida State back. Needing to go 80 yards to score the winning touchdown, Winston went to work. He hit Rashad Greene on back-to-back pass plays for 8 and 49 yards, driving the Seminoles to the Auburn 23. He completed a pass to running back Devonta Freeman down to the 17 and called time out with 46 seconds to play. Two more completions moved Florida State to the Auburn 5-yard line. They were called for a delay of game, which moved the ball back to the 10. Facing third-and-8, Winston's pass fell incomplete but Chris Davis, who was the hero in the Iron Bowl against Alabama, was

Wide receiver Marcus Nash of the Tennessee Volunteers gets tackled by linebacker Tony Oritz of the Nebraska Cornhuskers during the Orange Bowl

ged for pass interference, giving the ball first-and-goal for Florida State at the Auburn 2-yard line. Winston hit Kelvin Benjamin for the score with 13 seconds to play to give Florida State a 34-31 win and end the seven-year run of the SEC.

Oklahoma (2000), Miami (FL) (2001), Ohio State (2002), USC (2004, though they had to vacate the BCS national title as part of NCAA sanctions), Texas (2005), and Florida State (2013) also won championships in the BCS era.

2014: THE COLLEGE FOOTBALL PLAYOFF TAKES OVER FOR THE BCS

The 2013 BCS national championship game proved to be the final BCS title contest in the history of the sport. The NCAA had voted in 2013 to scrap the BCS format and its potential controversy in order to go to a four-team playoff. The College Football Playoff, as it was officially named, began in the 2014 season. The four teams selected to play are chosen by a committee of 13 individuals, including one current athletic director from schools in the Big Ten, ACC, SEC, Big 12, and Pac-12 Conferences in addition to former coaches, players, administrators, or athletic directors. There will be rotation of personnel in the roles; the first terms expire in 2016 with others coming up in 2017 and 2018.

Instead of computers and polls determining the top teams in the country, the committee makes the decision based on a variety of criteria. Strength of schedule is widely considered to be a major factor, to prevent top-tier teams from beating up on poor clubs in an effort to pad their statistics. Conference titles, head-to-head records against other opponents, along with factors like weather and injuries that may have helped or impeded a team's performance are also considered. Teams are seeded one through four with the top-seeded team facing the fourth-seeded team and the second

Quarterback Jameis Winston of the Florida State Seminoles celebrates after a 2-yard pass for a touchdown to take a 33-31 lead over the Auburn Tigers during the 2014 Vizio BCS national championship game on January 6, 2014, in Pasadena, CA.

seed playing the third in the semifinal round. The winners of those two contests move on to play the college football championship game.

Six bowl games comprise the rotation for the semifinal games of the College Football Playoff: the Rose, Fiesta, Sugar, Orange, Cotton, and Chick-fil-A Peach Bowls. The Rose and Sugar Bowls were the inaugural semifinal games for the College Football Playoff on January 1, 2015, while the Orange and Cotton Bowls will make their College Football Playoff debuts on December 31, 2015, and the Fiesta and Chick-fil-A Peach Bowls will debut on December 31, 2016. The bowls will rotate every three seasons. The first college football championship game was held on January 12, 2015, at Cowboys Stadium in Arlington, Texas, and the 2015 championship game will be held January 11, 2016, at the University of Phoenix Stadium in Glendale, Arizona. The 2016 championship game will be held on January 9, 2017, at Raymond James Stadium in Tampa, Florida.

This format will determine the champion of college football through at least the 2025 season. ESPN paid a reported $7.3 billion to get the television rights for all of the College Football Playoff games, while Dr. Pepper will be the sponsor for the College Football Playoff National Championship Trophy; they shelled out a reported $35 million for the rights through the 2020 season.

The first season of the College Football Playoff was historic as it made a team win two games during bowl season to become the national champions. While there are many proponents of the system, the inevitable fact is that at least one of the five power conferences will be slighted each year if the playoff field remains limited to four teams. In 2014 that meant the Big 12 Conference ended up on the outside looking in for the playoff as #1 Alabama, #2 Oregon, #3 Florida State, and #4 Ohio State comprised the field. Ohio State qualified in the final release of the rankings after destroying Wisconsin 59-0 in the Big Ten championship game.

Linebacker Tony Washington (#91) of the Oregon Ducks runs back a fumble by quarterback Jameis Winston of the Florida State Seminoles for a 58-yard touchdown in the third quarter of the College Football Playoff semifinal at the Rose Bowl game on January 1, 2015, in Pasadena, CA.

That Ohio State triumph that pushed them into the College Football Playoff took both Baylor and TCU of the Big 12 out of the picture. The two teams were co-champions of the conference, though Baylor won the head-to-head matchup 61-58 in one of the most entertaining games of the year. TCU had been #3 in the rankings the week before the Big Ten championship game while Baylor was #6; even with TCU walloping Iowa State 55-3 and Baylor beating #9 Kansas State 38-27, they were unable to stay in the playoffs. The prevailing opinion that came out from the committee after those final rankings was that TCU and Baylor were hurt by the lack of a conference championship game as each of the other four power conferences (ACC, SEC, Big Ten, and Pac-12) have one. As it turned out, the winner of each of those conference championship games went on to the College Football Playoff.

In the Rose Bowl, which served as one of the two semifinal games for the College Football Playoff, there was a matchup of the last two Heisman Trophy winners as Marcus Mariota, the 2014 winner, led Oregon against Jameis Winston and Florida State. The Seminoles entered the game on a 29-game win streak but they failed to measure up against the Ducks. Mariota threw for 338 yards and two touchdowns while running for 62 more plus a score as Oregon hammered Florida State 59-20. Oregon rolled up 639 yards of offense and forced five Florida State turnovers. They scored the final 34 points of the game to pull away.

Meanwhile, in the Sugar Bowl, top-ranked Alabama seemed to have a major edge over #4 Ohio State, who was down to their third-string quarterback in Cardale Jones after Braxton Miller was injured before the season and J.T. Barrett broke his ankle against Michigan in late November. Jones led Ohio State to the win over Wisconsin and helped rally his team from a 21-6 deficit in the Sugar Bowl, and the Buckeyes ended up taking a 42-35 victory. Jones threw for 243 yards plus a score while Ezekiel Elliott ran

Cardale Jones (#12) of the Ohio State Buckeyes looks to pass the ball against the Wisconsin Badgers during the Big Ten championship on December 6, 2014, in Indianapolis, IN.

for 230 yards and two touchdowns in the game, setting up the showdown with Oregon for the national title.

In the national championship game, a team no one thought would be there ended up being the first College Football Playoff national champion as Ohio State, despite turning the ball over four times, whipped Oregon 42-20. Jones did a solid job managing the game as he was 16 of 23 throwing the ball for 242 yards with a touchdown and an interception plus 38 yards and a score on the ground. Elliott did the damage on the ground, carrying the ball 36 times for 246 yards and four scores. Ohio State's defense held Oregon to 2 of 12 on third down to thwart drives. Mariota, in his final college game, completed 24 of 37 passes for 333 yards with two touchdowns and one interception; he declared for the 2015 NFL Draft on January 15, 2015.

A HISTORY OF FIRSTS

No matter how many times a record or a milestone is reached or broken, there had to be someone that did it first. There have been plenty of 1,000-yard rushing seasons in college football, or 3,000-yard passing campaigns, but the very first time these feats

Ezekiel Elliott (#15) of th
touchdown agai
Sugar B

were achieved, especially in the era when offenses weren't quite as sophisticated or powerful as they are these days, carried far greater weight.

For example, college football did not have its first 1,500-yard rusher until 1948, when Fred Wendt of Texas Mines, now the University of Texas-El Paso, ran for 1,570 yards. College football's first 2,000-yard pass came the same season, as Nevada's Stan Heath threw for 2,005 yards to a 9-2 mark, though they lost the Harbor Bowl that year 27-7 to Villanova. Ernie Davis was the first African American to claim the Heisman Trophy in 1961, while Archie Griffin was the first two-time winner of the Heisman Trophy when he claimed the award in 1974 and 1975. To date, Griffin is still the only two-time winner of the Heisman Trophy.

Tulsa's Bill Anderson was the first quarterback in history to break the 3,000-yard passing plateau in college when he threw for 3,464 yards in 1965. USC's star running back Mike Garrett, who won the Heisman Trophy that season, became the first Heisman winner to lead the nation in rushing the year they won the award. Emory Ballard, the offensive coordinator at the University of Texas, unveiled the wishbone formation. After Texas rung up 30 straight victories beginning in 1968, the wishbone became all the rage among college offenses.

In 1971, Cornell running back Ed Marinaro would become the first player in NCAA history to average 200 yards rushing per game in a season, as he averaged 209 for the Big Red, running for 1,881 yards in nine games for Cornell, who went 8-1 on the season. Marinaro finished second in the Heisman Trophy voting that year to Auburn quarterback Pat Sullivan. A decade later in 1981, USC's Marcus Allen was college football's first 2,000-yard rusher in a season when he ran for 2,382 yards and won the Heisman Trophy for the Trojans. Brian Westbrook was the first player to have 1,000 yards rushing and 1,000 yards receiving in the same season in 1998 while at Villanova. Tim Tebow of Florida was the first sophomore to win the Heisman Trophy when he

Quarterback Marcus Mariota (#8) of the Oregon Ducks reacts to a play against the Ohio State Buckeyes during the College Football Playoff national championship game on January 12, 2015, in Arlington, TX.

claimed the award in 2007. Paul Hornung of Notre Dame was the first and, to date, only player to ever win the Heisman on a losing team when he claimed the award in 1956.

The first indoor college game was the 1896 Thanksgiving Day clash between Michigan and the University of Chicago that took place in the Chicago Coliseum; in 1903 Harvard built the first large, permanent football stadium, known as Harvard Stadium. Michigan's 49-0 win over Stanford in the 1902 East-West Football Classic was the first bowl game in college football history. It would be renamed the Rose Bowl in 1923 when the game began being contested within the newly built Rose Bowl stadium in Pasadena, California.

The first televised college football game took place in 1939 between Fordham and Waynesburg, with Fordham victorious by a score of 34-7. The first nationally televised contest was the 1952 Rose Bowl, which saw Illinois pummel Stanford by a score of 40-7, while the first nationally televised regular season clash came the following year, when Kansas blanked TCU by a score of 13-0. Minnesota's 21-3 victory over UCLA in the 1962 Rose Bowl marked the first nationally broadcast game in color, while the 1963 Army/Navy clash was the first time that instant replay was used in a telecast. Alabama's 33-32 victory over Ole Miss in 1969 marked the first nationally televised game in prime time.

The first pair of teammates to win the Heisman Trophy in back-to-back seasons was Larry Kelley and Clint Frank for Yale. Kelley won it in 1936 and Frank followed in 1937. Of course, when it comes to the Heisman, Jay Berwanger of Chicago was the first to win it, when it was still known as the Downtown Athletic Club Trophy, in 1935. Minnesota was the first national champion in the Associated Press poll in 1936, while Bud Wilkinson's Oklahoma squad was the first UPI-chosen national champion in 1950.

Texas A&I's 37-15 walloping of UTEP in 1981 marked the first time a Division II school beat a Division I-A program in college football history. Meanwhile, Appalachian State's stunning

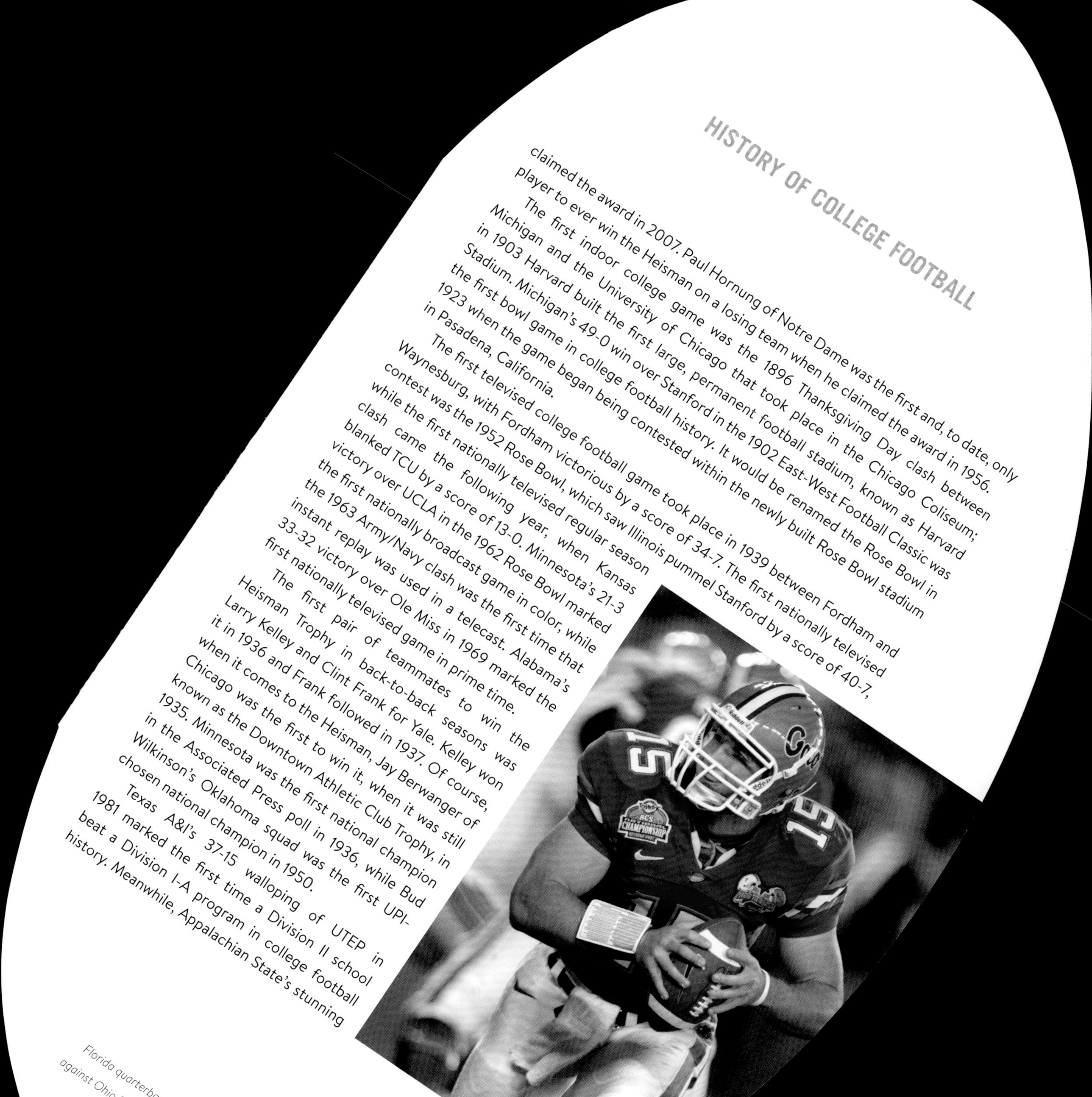

Florida quarterbo
against Ohio

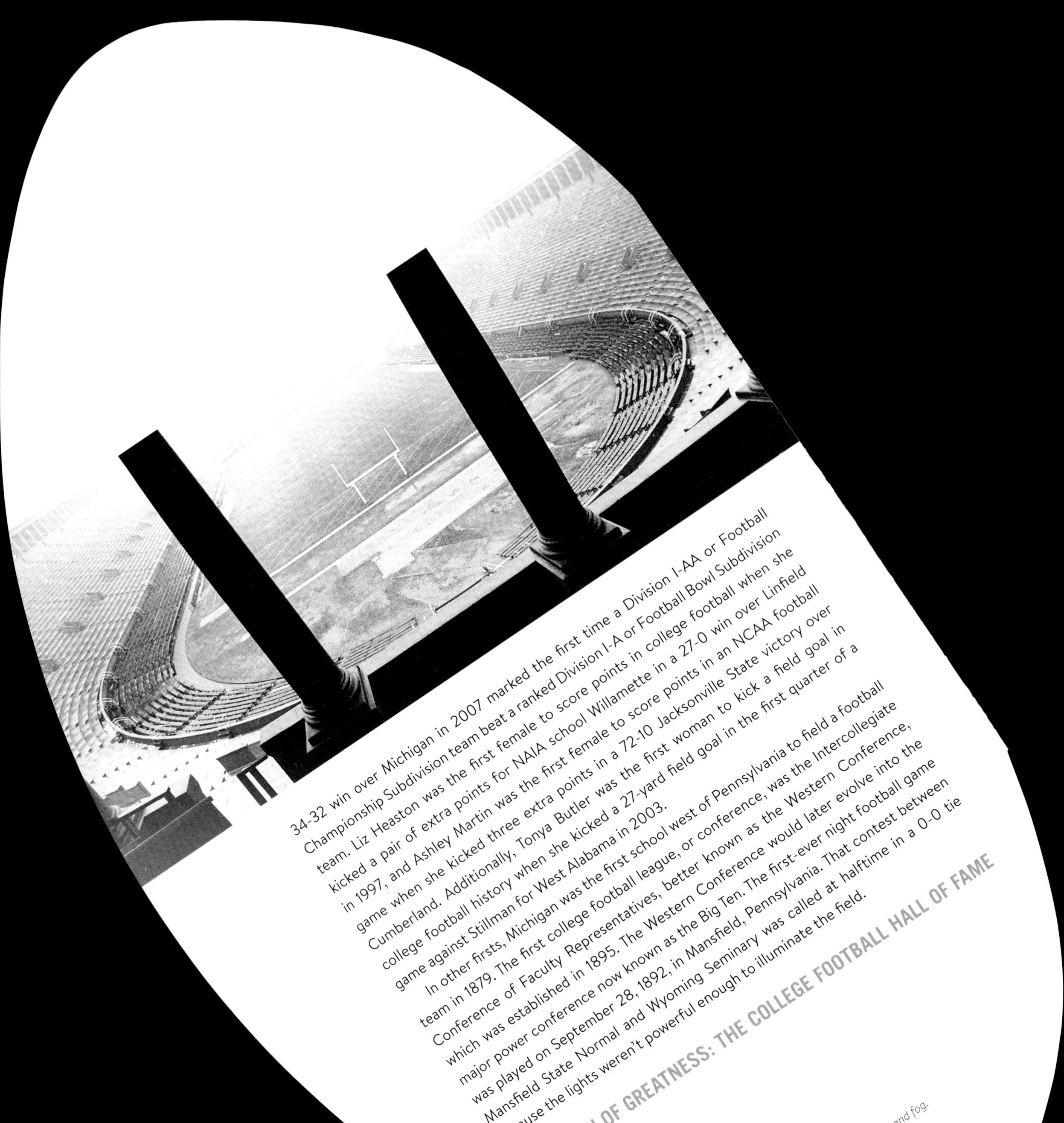

34-32 win over Michigan in 2007 marked the first time a Division I-AA or Football Championship Subdivision team beat a ranked Division I-A or Football Bowl Subdivision team. Liz Heaston was the first female to score points in college football when she kicked a pair of extra points for NAIA school Willamette in a 27-0 win over Linfield in 1997, and Ashley Martin was the first female to score points in an NCAA football game when she kicked three extra points in a 72-10 Jacksonville State victory over Cumberland. Additionally, Tonya Butler was the first woman to kick a field goal in college football history when she kicked a 27-yard field goal in the first quarter of a game against Stillman for West Alabama in 2003.

In other firsts, Michigan was the first school west of Pennsylvania to field a football team in 1879. The first college football league, or conference, was the Intercollegiate Conference of Faculty Representatives, better known as the Western Conference, which was established in 1895. The Western Conference would later evolve into the major power conference now known as the Big Ten. The first-ever night football game was played on September 28, 1892, in Mansfield, Pennsylvania. That contest between Mansfield State Normal and Wyoming Seminary was called at halftime in a 0-0 tie use the lights weren't powerful enough to illuminate the field.

OF GREATNESS: THE COLLEGE FOOTBALL HALL OF FAME

and fog.

HISTORY OF COLLEGE FOOTBALL

The ultimate goal of any athlete is to be known as one of the best to ever play the sport. In this instance, that would mean being inducted to the College Football Hall of Fame. Of the nearly five million people who have played college football since the sport became a reality, 934 have had their names called to be inducted. Meanwhile, only 205 coaches have had their likenesses enshrined in the College Football Hall of Fame. It's an accolade that truly is reserved for the absolute best of the best.

There are several strict criteria in order to even be considered for induction. For players, they must have received the accolade of being a first-team All-American selection during some point in their career. They also must have completed their college career at least 10 years prior to enshrinement. This means that an athlete who finished playing college football in 1994 would not be eligible to be enshrined until at least 2004. By the same token, a player who is still playing professionally may not be enshrined. Doug Flutie is a prime example of this. His career at Boston College ended in 1984, which would have made him eligible to be inducted starting in 1994. However, his professional career did not end until the 2006 season, meaning he was ineligible to be selected until 2007. The Hall of Fame also considers what an athlete does after playing college football. Finally, the player's final year of college football must have been played in the last 50 years. For example, a player who is eligible for the 2013 induction class would have had to play college football last in 1963 or later. Players who fall outside this purview can be selected by the Division I-A and the Divisional Honors Review boards.

There are set standards for the induction of coaches as well. A coach must have coached for at least 10 years in the college ranks and compiled a winning percentage of at least .600 over the course of 100 games or more. What coaches do after their coaching days are over is taken into consideration as

Defensive tackle Terrance Talyor (#67) and linebacker Shawn Crable (#2) of the Michigan Wolverines tackle running back Kevin Richardson (#28) of the Appalachian State Mountaineers on September 1, 2007, in Ann Arbor, MI.

well. Coaches are eligible for enshrinement three years after they retire from the coaching ranks, or immediately if they retire at or after age 70. A coach actively coaching at age 75 is eligible for induction even without retiring. As with players, coaches who fall short of the above listed criteria may end up being inducted through the Division I-A or Divisional Honors Review boards. Gene Stallings was a prime example of this method of induction. He was inducted in 2011 despite a record of 89-70-1 (.559 winning percentage). He did post a mark of 62-25 (.713 winning percentage) and won a national championship while at Alabama, however.

Notre Dame is the school that is most represented in the College Football Hall of Fame: as of the 2015 induction class, the Fighting Irish have had 45 players inducted. The Michigan Wolverines are second with 32 Hall of Fame inductees, while USC (31 inductees), Yale (25), and Army (24) round out the top five most represented schools. In addition, Ohio State has had 24 players inducted; Princeton and Oklahoma have had 21 inductees; while Alabama, Navy, and Tennessee each have seen 20 players inducted to the Hall of Fame since its inception in 1951. To date, a total of 963 players and 209 coaches have been enshrined into the College Football Hall of Fame, representing a total of 302 schools.

Originally, the College Football Hall of Fame was slated to be built on the campus of Rutgers University, as it was the venue for the first game in college football history. That never panned out and the first Hall of Fame opened in 1978 in Kings Mills, Ohio. Attendance dwindled as time went by and the venue was closed for good in 1992. A new venue for the Hall of Fame opened in 1995 in

Quarterback Doug Flutie (#7) of the Buffalo Bills in action during a game against the New England Patriots at the Rich Stadium in

South Bend, Indiana, two miles (3.2km) south of the campus of the University of Notre Dame. It closed on December 30, 2012, after it, too, failed to draw as many visitors as originally projected.

The newest location for the College Football Hall of Fame is in Atlanta, Georgia. The $68 million project is near the Centennial Olympic Park, which was a focal point in the 1996 Summer Olympics held in the city, and is nearly 95,000 square feet (8,826 m^2). It opened in August 2014.

OPTIONS AFTER COLLEGE FOOTBALL

Ideally, the goal of every major college football player is to play professionally. The National Football League is the top rung of the professional ladder. Ultimately, only a very small percentage of college football players realize this dream. The NFL draft is only seven rounds, with compensatory picks factored in as well. This means that roughly 250 players out of all the players who either declare for the NFL Draft before using all their college eligibility or those who have finished their collegiate careers are chosen. Others may catch on as undrafted free agents, or practice squad players.

The average span of a professional career in the NFL is only slightly over three years. That number goes up for players who make the opening day roster in their rookie season to an average of six years. The average career span of a first-round draft pick is 9.3 years and should a player be selected to a Pro Bowl, the average career length extends to 11.7 years. Those numbers are misleading, however, because they eliminate players who don't make the active roster as a rookie, practice squad players, and the rest.

Should a player not make it in the NFL, there are other options available. The Canadian Football

Alabama head coach Gene Stallings stands on the field with his team before the Crimson Tide's 17-13 victory over the Tennessee

League, which is comprised of eight teams across Canada, tends to have an American influence as far as the personnel. Hall of Fame quarterback Warren Moon honed his craft with the Edmonton Eskimos for six years before finally getting a crack at the NFL. Doug Flutie, chased out of the NFL because of his size, had tremendous success in Canada and then returned to the NFL to play with the Buffalo Bills, San Diego Chargers, and New England Patriots. The change in rules (three downs instead of four, 12 players instead of 11 on the field at one time, along with a longer, wider field and scoring variations) can be something to adapt to, but the option is viable should a player be interested in pursuing it.

There also is the Arena Football League, which has its own conventions to adjust to. Players tend to play both ways, the field is only 50 yards long, the goalposts are narrower (9 feet (2.74m) as opposed to 18'6" (5.64m) in the NFL) and higher (the crossbar is 15 feet (4.57m) instead of 10 feet (3.05m)) while the running game is nearly nonexistent. Factor in that there are walls on the sides of the field and that games normally end up with scores that look like video games and it's quite a change. Don't expect to get rich playing in the Arena League; players make $830 per game under the league's collective bargaining agreement.

Given the low percentage of players who go on to have successful, lucrative professional careers, it is always advised that student athletes pursue and complete a college degree to have an alternative career path should their playing career prove to

ABOVE: *Warren Moon of the Houston Oilers.*

RIGHT: *Tight end Nick Vannett (#81) of the Ohio State Buckeyes celebrates with the trophy after defeating the Oregon Ducks 42-20 in the College Football Playoff national championship game at AT&T Stadium on January 12, 2015, in Arlington, TX.*

UNDISPUTED
NATIONAL
CHAMPIONS
2015

12

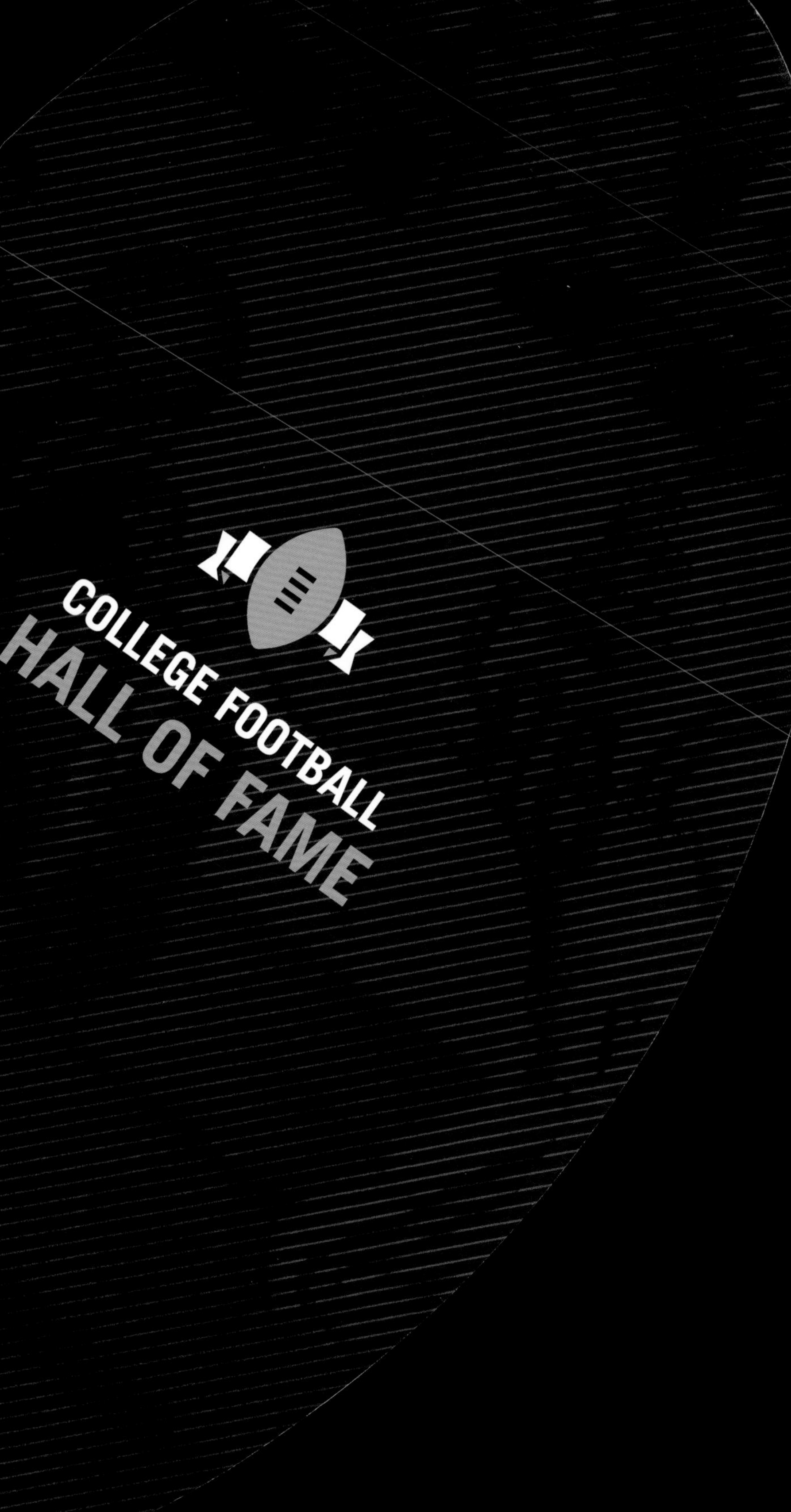
COLLEGE FOOTBALL
HALL OF FAME

MARCUS ALLEN

BORN: MARCH 26, 1960, IN SAN DIEGO, CALIFORNIA
HEIGHT: 6'2" (1.88 M) | WEIGHT: 202 LB (92 KG) | POSITION: RUNNING BACK
TEAM: UNIVERSITY OF SOUTHERN CALIFORNIA TROJANS
ACHIEVEMENTS: CONSENSUS ALL-AMERICAN (1981), HEISMAN TROPHY (1981)
INDUCTED INTO THE COLLEGE FOOTBALL HALL OF FAME IN 2000

Marcus Allen was a fantastic running back who continued the tradition of great runners coming from the University of Southern California. The school had already produced Mike Garrett, O.J. Simpson, Sam Cunningham, and Charles White; Allen followed in the footsteps of these elite college backs and made a name for himself as well. Allen claimed the Heisman in his senior season of 1981, adding another Heisman Trophy to the USC collection.

Allen played at USC from 1978 to 1981 and after a slow start his freshman and sophomore years, really got going in his final two seasons at the school. This can be attributed to playing behind 1979 Heisman Trophy winner Charles White in those first two seasons. Allen finished his career with 893 carries for 4,682 yards and 45 rushing touchdowns, and added 79 receptions for an additional 721 yards and a touchdown. Allen's elusiveness and speed often allowed him to break containment and turn short runs into long gains.

As said, Allen didn't see a lot of work in his freshman season of 1978 at USC. He carried the ball just 31 times for 171 yards and a touchdown. Allen was actually well down the depth chart his freshman season, as White (342 carries, 1,760 yards and 12 touchdowns) and Lynn Cain (187 carries, 977 yards, four touchdowns) combined for 2,737 yards on the ground and 16 scores on their own. USC finished the season with a 12-1 mark, with their lone defeat coming in mid-October when Arizona State turned the Trojans away 20-7. USC rallied to win their final eight games, including a 17-10 victory over Michigan in the Rose Bowl. USC claimed part of a split national championship: Alabama won the AP championship, while USC was the champion in the UPI, or the coaches' poll.

Allen's sophomore season saw him get more work due to the departure of Cain from the depth chart. While White still took the bulk of the carries (293 carries, 1,803 yards, 18 touchdowns), Allen carried the ball 105 times and gained a total of 606 yards while scoring eight rushing touchdowns. He added 20 receptions for an additional 273 yards as well. USC began the season as the top team in the nation and held that ranking into mid-October. A 21-21 tie with Stanford knocked them from the top spot and they

Marcus Allen (#32) of the Los Angeles Raiders carries the ball against the Pittsburgh Steelers in a 1983 AFC divisional playoff game at the Los Angeles Memorial Coliseum on January 1, 1984, in Los Angeles, CA. The Raiders defeated the Steelers 38-10.

were unable to recapture the #1 ranking the rest of the season. It would prove to be the only blemish on their record. USC finished the year 11-0-1, capped by a 17-16 win in the Rose Bowl over Ohio State.

Allen's junior year in 1980 was the first season that he was the unquestioned starter in the Trojans' backfield, and coach John Robinson wasted no time in sticking to the strategy of running the ball down opposing teams' throats. After carrying the ball a total of 136 times in his first two seasons, Allen saw that number more than double in 1980, as he became the workhorse back for USC. Allen carried the ball 354 times for 1,563 yards and 14 touchdowns. He also added an additional 231 yards on 30 receptions. USC finished the year 8-2-1, with two late losses to Washington and UCLA sending the Trojans tumbling from the #2 ranking in the nation to as low as #17. A season-ending victory over then #2 Notre Dame vaulted them to 11th in the final polls of the season.

Allen's senior year in 1981 was nothing short of spectacular. He was the focal point of the USC offense, and even with opposing defenses knowing that number 33 was going to get the ball, they seemed powerless to stop him. Allen carried the ball a staggering 403 times for 2,342 yards and 22 touchdowns, while adding 29 receptions for another 217 yards and a score. For his efforts, he was named a consensus All-American selection and claimed the Heisman Trophy, USC's second in three years (White won it in 1979). USC was the #1 team in the nation for three weeks, but a 13-10 loss to Arizona quashed that. The Trojans finished the year 9-3 and lost in the Fiesta Bowl 26-10 to Penn State. The Trojans finished 14th in the final Associated Press poll.

His college career over, Allen was selected in the first round with the 10th overall selection of the 1982 NFL Draft by the Los Angeles Raiders. During his NFL career, which ended in 1997, Allen was the Offensive Rookie of the Year (1982), Super Bowl MVP (1983), NFL MVP (1985), NFL Offensive Player of the Year (1985) and NFL Comeback Player of the Year (1993). He spent 11 seasons with the Raiders before going to division rival Kansas City in 1993 and playing with the Chiefs for the remainder of his career.

Allen finished his career with 3,022 carries for 12,243 yards and 123 touchdowns on the ground. He also added 587 receptions for an additional 5,411 yards and 21 receiving scores. Allen retired after the 1997 season. He was inducted into the Pro Football Hall of Fame in 2003 after being inducted into the College Football Hall of Fame in 2000. USC retired his number 33 following his college career.

Portrait of Marcus Allen in his University of Southern California Trojans uniform, Los Angeles, CA, 1979.

33
33
33
BIKE
BIKE

BAUGH

...: MARCH 17, 1914, IN TEMPLE, TEXAS
...88 M) | WEIGHT: 180 LB (82 KG) | POSITION: HALFBACK
...AM: TEXAS CHRISTIAN UNIVERSITY HORNED FROGS
ACHIEVEMENTS: CONSENSUS ALL-AMERICAN (1936)
INDUCTED INTO THE COLLEGE FOOTBALL HALL OF FAME IN 1951

Slinging Sammy Baugh was one of the greatest triple-threat players of his generation. He was capable of beating opposing defenses with his arm, his running ability, or by playing field position through punts. There were few who could match his ability, both in college and in the National Football League. His numbers are awe inspiring, and his talent was breathtaking to watch.

Baugh played three years in college, from 1934 through 1936, at Texas Christian University, better known as TCU. For his career, Baugh completed 270 of 587 passes (46 percent completion rate) for 3,384 yards with 39 touchdown passes and 54 interceptions. He ran the ball 158 times for 372 yards and five touchdowns, added three receptions for 23 yards, and punted 198 times for a 40.9-yard average. Baugh also intercepted 10 passes on defense, averaged 12.4 yards on 80 punt returns and 14 yards on a pair of kickoff returns.

Baugh played three sports at TCU—football, baseball, and basketball—but ultimately football would be his path to greatness. In 1934, his first year with the team, Baugh took over as the starting quarterback for the program. He completed 69 of 171 passes (40.4 percent completion rate) for 883 yards with 11 touchdown passes and 19 interceptions. Baugh added 114 yards on 44 rushing attempts with two touchdowns and 23 more yards on three receptions. In the kicking game, he punted 43 times and averaged 42.3 yards per punt. He also averaged 10.8 yards on 13 punt returns and had a 22-yard kickoff return. Baugh intercepted three passes on defense as well. TCU finished the 1934 season with an 8-4 record.

The 1935 season saw improvement for Baugh in the passing game. He completed 97 of 210 pass attempts (46.2 percent completion rate) for 1,240 yards, 18 touchdown passes, and 17 interceptions. Baugh added 195 rushing yards and three scores on 60 rushing attempts. He was impressive in the kicking department again, as he averaged 43 yards on 66 punts. Baugh averaged 14.1 yards on 28 punt returns and also ran a kickoff 6 yards. Baugh helped on defense, intercepting a pair of passes and returning them 25 yards. TCU finished the season 12-1, their lone defeat a 20-13 loss to SMU in the next-to-last regular season contest. TCU closed out the season with a 3-2 win over LSU in the Sugar Bowl.

Washington Redskins Hall of Fame quarterback Sammy Baugh.

HALL OF FAMER: SAMMY BAUGH

The 1936 season was Baugh's last at TCU. He continued to make strides as a passer, completing 104 of 206 passes (50.5 percent completion rate) for 1,261 yards with 10 touchdown passes and 18 interceptions. Baugh added 63 yards on 54 carries on the ground. He punted the ball 89 times, averaging 38.8 yards per kick, and averaged 11.7 yards on 39 punt returns. Baugh also added five interceptions on defense, the best total he posted as a collegian. TCU finished 9-2-2 on the season, including a 16-6 victory over Marquette in the first-ever Cotton Bowl. Baugh was named the MVP of that contest. He also was named a consensus All-American selection and finished fourth in the Heisman Trophy voting, which was won by Yale's Larry Kelley.

After his college career, Baugh was selected with the sixth overall selection in the 1937 NFL Draft by the Washington Redskins. Baugh played for the franchise through 1952 before retiring. He was a seven-time first-team All-Pro selection, was named Player of the Year in 1947 and 1948, and would go on to be named to both the NFL's All-Decade team of the 1940s and the 75th Anniversary team. Baugh completed 1,693 of 2,995 passes (56.5 percent completion rate) for 21,886 yards, 187 touchdown passes, and 203 interceptions. He additionally led the league in punting four straight years, and he is the only player in NFL history to lead the league in passing, punting and interceptions in the same season. Baugh was inducted into the College Football Hall of Fame in 1951 and was one of the 17 members of the charter class of the Pro Football Hall of Fame in 1963. Baugh's number 33 was retired by the Washington Redskins; it remains the only number retired by the franchise in its history.

throws a

JIM BROWN

BORN: FEBRUARY 17, 1936, IN ST. SIMONS, GEORGIA
HEIGHT: 6'2" (1.88 M) | WEIGHT: 212 LB (96 KG) | POSITION: HALFBACK
TEAM: SYRACUSE UNIVERSITY ORANGEMEN
ACHIEVEMENTS: CONSENSUS ALL-AMERICAN (1956)
INDUCTED INTO THE COLLEGE FOOTBALL HALL OF FAME IN 1995

Jim Brown was as dominant a running back as both college and professional football have arguably ever seen. He was a force to be reckoned with that went far beyond the white lines of the football field. While Brown was at Syracuse, he also thrived in basketball, track and field, and lacrosse. He earned second-team All-American honors as a lacrosse player and twice averaged better than 11 points a game on the basketball court.

...est known for his bruising, punishing style of running. He ran for 2,061 ...seasons at Syracuse, including a total of 986 yards in just eight ...season of 1964. Brown averaged 5.8 yards per carry, and ...er kickoff return in his career at the school as well. He ...d on defense, recording eight interceptions while

...hing as a sophomore in 1954 as he ran 75 ...es that season and kicked a pair of ...k. They dropped three straight ...final four games in order ...r as the focal ...66 yards. ...the

ny
32
28
60

collegiate game. Ultimately, the Orangemen would fall short, losing 28-27 to TCU thanks to a blocked extra point in the Cotton Bowl. Syracuse would finish the year with a 7-2 mark as the eighth-ranked team in the nation.

Brown would be named a consensus All-American selection in 1956 for his performance. He also finished fifth in the Heisman Trophy voting that year; Paul Hornung of Notre Dame would win the Heisman. Hornung went on to have a Hall of Fame career of his own in the NFL while playing for the Green Bay Packers.

Brown would become eligible for the NFL Draft following the completion of the 1956 college season. Cleveland Browns pounced on the opportunity ... talented running back, taking him with ... all selection in the 1956 NFL Draft. ... but for the team in 1957, and in ... eer that ended in 1965, he ... ight times. Brown was ... all of Fame in 1971 ... in 1995. He is

70
25

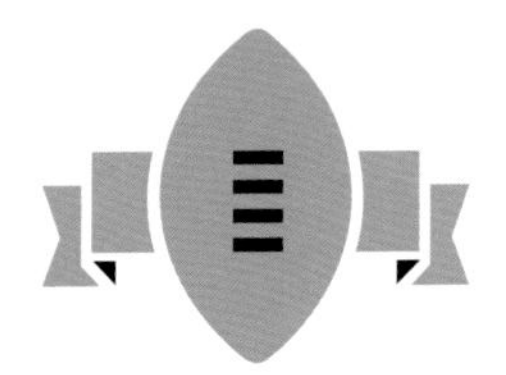

DICK BUTKUS

BORN: DECEMBER 9, 1942, IN CHICAGO, ILLINOIS
HEIGHT: 6'3" (1.91M) | WEIGHT: 237 LB (108 KG) | POSITION: CENTER
TEAM: UNIVERSITY OF ILLINOIS FIGHTING ILLINI
ACHIEVEMENTS: CONSENSUS ALL-AMERICAN (1963, 1964)
INDUCTED INTO THE COLLEGE FOOTBALL HALL OF FAME IN 1983

Dick Butkus was a one-man wrecking crew for opposing offenses. It didn't matter whether offenses tried to go directly at him, or attempted to tailor their offensive scheme to go away from him, Butkus was there to make offensive progress difficult on fall Saturdays. He was a force on both sides of the ball, logging time as both an offensive lineman and a linebacker at the University of Illinois.

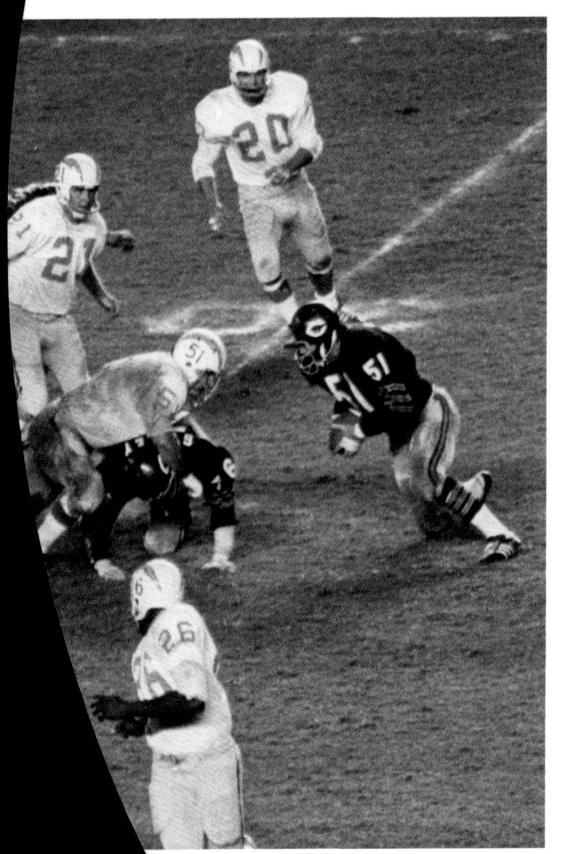

Butkus played three years for the Fighting Illini from 1962-64. The Illini were anything but a powerhouse in 1962, as the team was 2-7, finishing in the bottom 10 in all of Division I college football in both average points scored per game (8.3) and average points allowed per contest (26.0), in which they ranked 113th out of 120 teams.

In his career, Butkus totaled 374 tackles, which is still the eighth-best mark in school history. He intercepted five passes and had a 23-tackle performance against Ohio State in 1963. Butkus was named a consensus All-American selection in both 1963 and 1964 from his linebacker position and finished in the top six of the Heisman Trophy voting both years. This was almost unprecedented, as the Heisman Trophy tended to focus on offensive weapons rather than defensive stalwarts.

Butkus helped key a turnaround for the Illini in 1963, as the team finished the season with a record of 8-1-1 and the #3 ranking in the Associated Press poll. Butkus was at the heart of the Illinois defense, which cut points allowed per game from 26 in 1962 to a stingy 9.6 points per game in 1963, which was good for 17th in the nation. No Illinois opponent scored more than 21 points against them that season,

ABOVE: *Chicago Bears Hall of Fame linebacker Dick Butkus (#51) returns an interception during a preseason game in 1970.*
RIGHT: *Dick Butkus of the Chicago Bears awaits the next snap during a game on November 8, 1970, against the San Francisco 49ers at Wrigley Field in Chicago, IL.*

51
51

helping make up for a stagnant offensive attack. Butkus finished sixth in the Heisman voting in 1963 as Illinois won the Big Ten Conference and went on to beat Washington in the Rose Bowl by a count of 17-7.

The 1964 season saw the Illini backslide a bit, but Butkus was still playing at a high level. Illinois spent the first three weeks of the season ranked in the top five of the country, but a 26-0 shellacking by fourth-ranked Ohio State took the Illini out of the rankings for the rest of the season. They would get to 4-1, but back-to-back road losses to Purdue and Michigan knocked them down to 4-3. The team would close with shutout victories over Wisconsin and Michigan State, but the damage was done and there would be no bowl game for Illinois.

Butkus was again the linchpin for the Illini defense, which allowed just 11.1 points per game in 1964. Illinois' defense posted three shutouts and held two other opponents to seven points or less. For his efforts, Butkus finished third in the Heisman Trophy voting, trailing only John Huarte of Notre Dame and Jerry Rhome of Tulsa. He would turn professional following the 1964 college season.

With the NFL and the upstart American Football League in competition with each other, Butkus was selected in the first round of both the NFL and AFL drafts in 1965. The Chicago Bears took Butkus with one of their three first-round picks, while the Denver Broncos selected Butkus in the AFL Draft. Butkus signed with the Bears and spent his entire pro career with the team before retiring after sustaining several serious knee injuries after the 1973 season. He was inducted to the Pro Football Hall of Fame in 1979 and the College Football Hall of Fame in 1983.

Butkus had his jersey number 51 retired by the Chicago Bears and also had his number 50 retired by the University of Illinois. With that honor, Butkus is one of only two players in Illini history to have his number retired; the other is the legendary Red Grange (number 77).

Dick Butkus of the Chicago Bears at middle linebacker in an early 1970s NFL football game at Soldier Field in Chicago, IL.

51

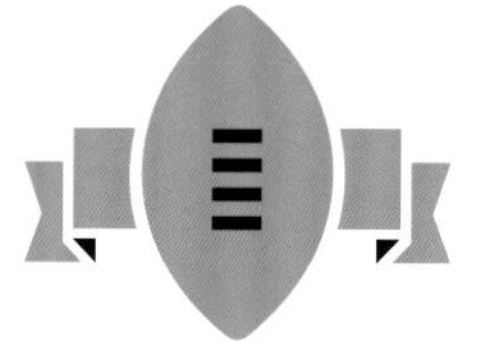

EARL CAMPBELL

BORN: MARCH 29, 1955, IN TYLER, TEXAS
HEIGHT: 5'11" (1.80 M) | WEIGHT: 220 LB (100 KG) | POSITION: RUNNING BACK
TEAM: UNIVERSITY OF TEXAS LONGHORNS
ACHIEVEMENTS: CONSENSUS ALL-AMERICAN (1977), HEISMAN TROPHY (1977)
INDUCTED INTO THE COLLEGE FOOTBALL HALL OF FAME IN 1990

Earl Campbell was a battering ram of a running back, capable of delivering a big hit and running over defenders as easily as he went around them. Campbell had no issue with going through someone to get enough yardage to move the sticks, or to put the ball in the end zone to help the University of Texas win football games. Campbell played four years at the school before turning pro.

Campbell played at Texas from 1974 to 1977. He twice rushed for over 1,000 yards at the school, and ended with a career total of 4,443 yards and 40 rushing touchdowns. He was a consensus All-American selection in 1977 and also claimed the Heisman Trophy that same year, which was his senior season. Texas was 34-12-1 in Campbell's four years at the school, though it was when Fred Akers took over for Darrell Royal that Campbell truly flourished.

The 1974 season was a solid debut campaign for Campbell in the Texas offense. He carried the ball 162 times for 928 yards and six touchdowns for the Longhorns. His rushing total led the team, and he was third in rushing touchdowns, trailing Marty Akins (10) and Graylon Wyatt (8), helping Texas become the seventh-highest scoring offense in the nation. After a slow start that saw Texas win just three of their first five games, the Longhorns won five of their final six regular season contests to go 8-3 and earn a berth in the Gator Bowl. In the end, Texas was no match for Auburn, which humbled Campbell and the Longhorns by a count of 27-3.

Campbell came back for his sophomore season in 1975 intent on keeping the momentum of his first season going. His numbers improved, as he carried the ball 198 times for 1,118 yards and 13 touchdowns. Campbell led the team in rushing attempts, rushing yards, and rushing touchdowns. Texas was the second-highest scoring offense in the nation in 1975 and finished 9-2 in the regular season. A loss to Texas A&M in the regular season finale sent the Longhorns to the Bluebonnet Bowl. Texas whipped Colorado 38-21 for their 10th victory of the season and they finished sixth in the final rankings.

The 1976 season saw Campbell regress a bit offensively in Darrell Royal's final season as the head coach at Texas. Campbell saw his carries drop from 198 to 138, his rushing yards drop from 1,118 to 653, and his rushing touchdown total drop from 13 to three in his junior year. Campbell still led the team in rushing attempts and yards, but

Texas Earl Campbell (#20) in action, rushing vs Oklahoma. Austin, TX

...ne from his numbers the first two seasons. After winning 18 ...wo years that Campbell was at the school, Texas slipped to 5-5-1 in ...ense fell from the second highest in the nation to 90th in 1976, and the ...y missed out on a bowl bid as well.

Campbell's senior season of 1977 saw a change at the top with the departure of Royal. Fred Akers took over the head coach position and he seemed intent on feeding Campbell the football on a regular basis. Campbell responded with his best season of his college career, carrying the ball 267 times for 1,844 yards and 18 rushing touchdowns. He added five receptions for 111 yards and another score out of the backfield in a limited passing attack for Texas. The performance paid off and rewarded Campbell with the Heisman Trophy. Campbell ran away from the field, dusting Terry Miller of Oklahoma State by 735 points to take the award. Texas won all 11 regular season games in the year, capturing the top ranking in the nation in late October and carrying it through the remainder of the regular season. With a chance at the national championship on the line, Texas was walloped by fifth-ranked Notre Dame by a score of 38-10 to knock them from the top spot. Texas ultimately finished fourth in the final rankings in 1977, and Campbell's collegiate career ended with a thud.

Campbell turned pro after the 1977 season and was selected by the Houston Oilers with the first overall pick of the 1978 NFL Draft. Campbell led the league in rushing three consecutive seasons from 1978 to 1980, making him the second back in NFL history to accomplish this feat. Campbell played for the Oilers from 1978 through part of the 1984 season. Houston dealt him to New Orleans partway through the 1984 season, where he was reunited with coach Bum Phillips. Campbell would play the rest of the 1984 and the 1985 season in a lesser role with the Saints before announcing his retirement during the 1986 preseason.

For his NFL career, Campbell was named to the Pro Bowl five times and ran for 9,407 yards with 74 rushing touchdowns. He eclipsed the 1,000-yard mark five times and was inducted into the Pro Football Hall of Fame in 1991. A year earlier, Campbell was recognized for his collegiate statistics, as he was inducted into the College Football Hall of Fame.

Texas Earl Campbell (#20) in action, rushing vs Oklahoma. Austin, TX.

ENN DAVIS

DECEMBER 26, 1924, IN CLAREMONT, CALIFORNIA
T: 5'9" (1.75 M) | WEIGHT: 170 LB (77 KG) | POSITION: HALFBACK
TEAM: UNITED STATES MILITARY ACADEMY ARMY BLACK KNIGHTS
ACHIEVEMENTS: CONSENSUS ALL-AMERICAN (1944, 1945, 1946), HEISMAN TROPHY (1946)
INDUCTED INTO THE COLLEGE FOOTBALL HALL OF FAME IN 1961

There simply may not have been as deadly a duo of running backs in the history of college football as the pairing of Glenn Davis and Doc Blanchard at Army in the mid-1940s. Army was 27-0-1 between 1944 and 1946 with both running backs in their lineup, and the duo racked up national awards and nicknames alike. Davis was "Mr. Outside" while Blanchard was "Mr. Inside." They combined to give defenses headaches on crisp fall Saturdays.

Davis played four years at Army, from 1943 to 1946. He was a consensus All- American selection three straight seasons from 1944 to 1946, won the Maxwell Award in 1944, and finished second in the Heisman voting in 1944 and 1945 before winning it in 1946. He finished his career with 2,957 yards rushing and 49 rushing touchdowns, to go along with 45 receptions for 850 yards and 10 additional scores. Davis completed 57 of 126 passes (45.2 percent completion rate) for 1,172 yards with 12 touchdowns and 14 interceptions. Davis also punted 22 times and intercepted 14 passes in his career at Army.

The 1943 season was the first for Davis at West Point, and the young man delivered on the football field. Davis carried the ball 95 times for 634 yards and seven touchdowns, while adding seven receptions for 68 yards and another score. Throwing the ball, he was 21 of 49 (42.9 percent completion rate) for 394 yards with four touchdown passes and five interceptions. He averaged 12 yards on 22 punt returns and 14 yards on a pair of kickoff returns and intercepted three passes as a freshman. Army finished the year with a record of 7-2-1 and a #11 ranking in the final Associated Press poll of the season.

The 1944 season saw the dominance of Davis and Blanchard as the duo began to unfold. Davis carried the ball just 58 times but ran for 667 yards, an average of 11.5 yards a carry, and 16 rushing touchdowns. He caught 13 passes out of the backfield for an additional 221 yards and four more touchdowns, giving him 20 on the season. Davis threw just 10 passes on the season, completing 6 for 129 yards with two touchdowns and one interception. He also averaged 18.4 yards on 16 punt returns and 29.5 yards on four kickoff returns. Defensively, Davis added four interceptions, which he returned for 92 yards. He won the Maxwell Award and finished second in the Heisman Trophy voting

United States Military Academy – West Point halfback Glenn Davis. Davis was the 1946 Heisman Trophy winner.

to Les Horvath of Ohio State. Blanchard, his teammate, finished third. Army finished the year with a perfect 9-0 record and was the Associated Press' national champion.

As dominant as Army was in 1944, they were just as brutal on opponents in 1945. The combination of Davis and Blanchard continued to give opposing defenses fits, and the Army defense made it difficult to score. Davis rushed the ball 82 times for 944 yards and 18 touchdowns, while adding an additional 213 yards on five receptions. He completed 11 of 20 passes (55 percent completion rate) for 253 yards with two touchdown passes and three interceptions. Davis averaged 10.5 yards on 22 punt returns and 27.5 yards on a pair of kick returns while intercepting a pair of passes on defense. He finished second in the Heisman voting again, this time to his teammate Blanchard. Army breezed through the schedule unscathed with another 9-0 record. They went wire-to-wire as the top team in the Associated Press poll and were named national champions for the second consecutive season.

The 1946 season was Davis' breakthrough year. After being stonewalled for the Heisman the two previous seasons, he claimed it in 1946. Davis carried the ball 123 times for 712 yards and eight touchdowns, while catching 20 passes for 348 yards and five more touchdowns. He also completed 19 of 47 passes (40.4 percent completion rate) for 396 yards with four touchdown passes and five interceptions. Davis punted the ball 19 times as a senior, averaged 11.3 yards on 24 punt returns and 38.5 yards on two kickoff returns. On defense, Davis was third on the team with five interceptions. Army was 9-0-1 on the season, the only marring of the record a scoreless tie with Notre Dame. A narrow three-point win over Navy in the season finale was enough to displace Army from the #1 ranking in the Associated Press polls; they finished second as the Irish claimed the top spot, no doubt helped by their 26-6 win over USC in their season finale.

Davis was selected with the second overall selection in the 1947 NFL Draft by the Detroit Lions, but never played for the franchise. He served three years in the United States Army before playing in the NFL with the Los Angeles Rams. Davis finished with 152 carries for 616 yards and four touchdowns, along with 50 receptions for 682 yards and five touchdowns in two seasons in the league. His career was cut short by a knee injury in 1952. Davis was inducted into the College Football Hall of Fame in 1961.

Glenn Davis, aka "Mr. Outside", an All-American halfback in the Army, poses on the field in his uniform.

41

DORSETT

: APRIL 7, 1954, IN ROCHESTER, PENNSYLVANIA
1" (1.80 M) | WEIGHT: 192 LB (87 KG) | POSITION: RUNNING BACK
TEAM: UNIVERSITY OF PITTSBURGH PANTHERS
CHIEVEMENTS: CONSENSUS ALL-AMERICAN (1976), HEISMAN TROPHY (1976)
INDUCTED INTO THE COLLEGE FOOTBALL HALL OF FAME IN 1994

Tony Dorsett was a tough, durable running back who had it all: explosiveness, durability, elusiveness, and drive. He spent four years at the University of Pittsburgh, breaking the 1,000-yard mark and double-digit rushing touchdowns in all four seasons at the school. He rushed for 6,082 yards and 55 touchdowns on the ground during his career.

Those numbers earned him a consensus All-American slot in 1976, a fourth-place finish in the Heisman race in 1975, and the Heisman Trophy in 1976. Dorsett also added the Maxwell Award and the Walter Camp Player of the Year Award to his trophy case in 1976 with his stellar performance. Dorsett was named to the first-team All-American team, though not a consensus selection, in 1973 and 1975, while being a second-team All-American selection in 1974.

Dorsett burst onto the scene in Pittsburgh as a freshman, becoming the first freshman player to be named a first-team All-American since Army's Doc Blanchard in 1944. Dorsett shredded opposing defenses, carrying the ball 288 times for 1,586 yards and a dozen rushing touchdowns while adding 12 receptions for an additional 84 yards. He helped lead Pitt to their first winning season in a decade as the team finished with a mark of 6-5-1, though they dropped three of their final four contests. Included in that slide was a 28-7 defeat at the hands of Arizona State in the Fiesta Bowl.

The 1974 season was another strong one for Dorsett as he posted his second straight 1,000-yard season and became the school's leading rusher, breaking the mark set by Marshall Goldberg. He would finish the year with 220 carries for 1,004 yards and 11 rushing touchdowns, while adding nine receptions for 58 yards. The team improved to a record of 7-4, but there was no bowl game in the cards for the Panthers as they dropped their final two regular season games to Notre Dame and Penn State.

Dorsett came back with a vengeance in 1975, setting the tone for a big year. He had 228 carries for 1,544 yards and 11 rushing touchdowns, while adding an additional 191 yards and three touchdowns on 11 receptions. Combining with fellow running back Elliott Walker, the duo accumulated nearly 2,500 yards on the ground and 19 rushing touchdowns. Pitt went 8-4 on the year and closed the season with a 33-19 victory over

Running back Tony Dorsett (#33) of the Dallas Cowboys rushes for yards during a 1985 NFC divisional playoff game against the Los Angeles Rams at Anaheim Stadium on January 4, 1996, in Anaheim, CA.

33

HALL OF FAMER: TONY DO

Kansas in the Sun Bowl. Dorsett set a school record when he ran for 303 yards ag Notre Dame, a game that Pitt won 34-20.

Dorsett's senior season was ultimately his finest campaign in his four years at the school. He carved up Notre Dame for 181 yards, Penn State for 224, and gashed Syracuse for 241 yards en route to becoming the first back in college football history to rush for at least 6,000 yards in a career. His numbers for his senior season were staggering: 338 carries for 1,948 yards and 21 touchdowns on the ground, while adding seven receptions for 73 yards and another touchdown as a receiver out of the backfield. The Heisman, Walter Camp, and Maxwell Awards were his in a landslide.

Even more important, Pitt went through the regular season undefeated, having turned aside all challengers. They rose to the #1 spot in the polls in early November and held the spot through the remainder of the regular season. They went to New Orleans to play in the Sugar Bowl against fifth-ranked Georgia with a chance at a national title. Dorsett would not let the school down, rushing for 202 yards as the Panthers handled the Bulldogs 27-3 to claim the national title and close Dorsett's college career on the highest of notes.

Dorsett would go on to the pros, as he was drafted by the Dallas Cowboys with the second overall selection in the 1977 NFL Draft. Dorsett played 11 years with the Cowboys, getting named to the Pro Bowl four times and winning a Super Bowl ring when the Cowboys turned aside the Denver Broncos in Super Bowl XII. He ran for 1,007 yards and 12 touchdowns as a rookie, earning him Rookie of the Year honors and making him the first player to win a national title one year and a Super Bowl the next.

Dorsett had eight 1,000-yard seasons in the National Football League, including a career-best mark of 1,646 yards in 1981. He finished his career with the Denver Broncos in 1988, leading the team with 703 yards on the ground before injuries took their toll, and he retired prior to the 1989 campaign.

Dorsett finished his career with 12,739 rushing yards and 77 rushing touchdowns. He also added 398 receptions for 3,554 yards and 13 additional scores. Dorsett was inducted into both the Pro Football Hall of Fame and the College Football Hall of Fame in 1994.

Tony Dorsett (#33) of the Pittsburgh Panthers on the field during a circa 1970s NCAA college football game. Dorsett played for the University of Pittsburgh from 1975-77.

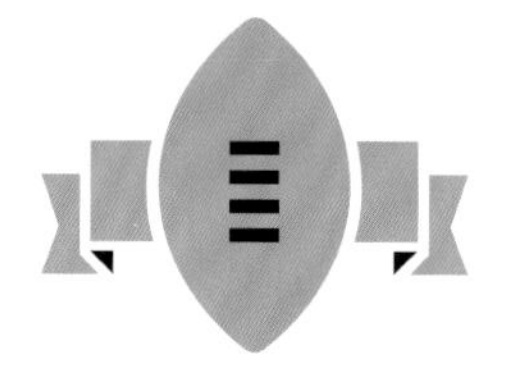

JOHN ELWAY

BORN: JUNE 28, 1960, IN PORT ANGELES, WASHINGTON
HEIGHT: 6'3" (1.91 M) | WEIGHT: 202 LB (92 KG) | POSITION: QUARTERBACK
TEAM: STANFORD UNIVERSITY CARDINAL
ACHIEVEMENTS: CONSENSUS ALL-AMERICAN (1982)
INDUCTED INTO THE COLLEGE FOOTBALL HALL OF FAME IN 2000

John Elway was a gun-slinging quarterback who was not afraid to use his cannon of an arm, or his legs, to make a big play on the field to help his team win a football game. Elway seemed to do just about everything possible in his four years at Stanford, except win a bowl game. From 1979-82, the Cardinal were a tough team to beat thanks to Elway's poise and leadership.

Elway was named the Pac-10 Player of the Year twice in his career (1980 and 1982) and also was a consensus All-American selection in 1982, which was his senior season. He finished second in the Heisman Trophy voting in 1982, losing to running back Herschel Walker of the Georgia Bulldogs. Andy Geiger, who was Stanford's athletic director at the time, made the assertion that Elway was robbed of the Heisman Trophy thanks to the improbable kick return through the Stanford band by their rivals, the California Golden Bears, in a game that is known for "The Play." Elway had driven the Cardinal downfield in the closing minutes to kick the go-ahead field goal with four seconds remaining before that took place.

Elway began his career in 1979 with Stanford. In his freshman season, Elway was not the starting quarterback, as he was behind Turk Schonert on the depth chart. Elway did complete 50 of 96 passes (52.1 percent completion rate) for 544 yards, six touchdowns and three interceptions. Stanford went 5-5-1 on the year, starting the season ranked 13th in the nation before a season-opening loss to Tulane. The high point of the year for Stanford was a 21-21 tie with then top-ranked USC on October 13.

Elway took over the starting quarterback role for Stanford beginning in 1980 as Schonert departed the program, having been selected in the ninth round of the 1980 NFL Draft by the Chicago Bears. Elway won his first Pac-10 Player of the Year Award that season, as he completed 65.4 percent of his passes for 2,889 yards with 27 touchdown passes against 11 interceptions. Stanford's offense averaged 28.4 points per game, which was good for 11th in the nation. Unfortunately, that prolific offensive assault did not translate into a bevy of victories. Stanford finished just 6-5 under Paul Wiggin, including a 28-23 defeat at the hands of rival Cal to close the season.

The 1981 season, which was Elway's junior year at Stanford, was another solid year for the developing quarterback. He completed 58.5 percent of his passes for 2,674 yards,

John Elway (#7) attempts a pass during a PAC-10 NCAA football game against the University of Oregon Ducks played on September 6, 1980, at Autzen Stadium in Eugene, OR.

Riddell
7

20 touchdowns, and 13 interceptions. The offense again did its job, posting an average of 28.5 points per contest, a number that was good for 16th in the nation. The defense was unable to stop anyone, however, and Stanford dropped six of their first seven contests. They rallied to win their final three games, including a 42-21 rout of Cal to finish 4-7.

Elway's senior season at Stanford led to his second Pac-10 Player of the Year Award as he was simply brilliant. Elway completed 64.7 percent of his passes for 3,242 yards to go with 24 touchdowns against just 12 interceptions. He was in the race for the Heisman Trophy before finishing second in that contest. He even showed a glimpse of what football fans would become accustomed to seeing in the NFL with a late fourth-quarter go-ahead drive against Cal. That the game ended up a defeat instead of a victory due to The Play should not diminish what Elway did. The loss to Cal did end Stanford's hopes of going to a bowl, as they finished 5-6, the losers of their final three contests.

Elway went on to the NFL, but not without a bit of controversy. The Baltimore Colts selected him with the first overall pick in the 1983 NFL Draft. Elway did not want to play for the franchise and, having played two seasons of minor league baseball in the New York Yankees organization, he threatened to play baseball full time if he was not dealt. The Colts ended up moving Elway to the Denver Broncos in exchange for Mark Herrmann, Chris Hinton, and a first-round pick in the 1984 NFL Draft.

Elway would go on to throw for 51,475 yards and 300 touchdowns in the NFL along with winning a pair of Super Bowl titles. He engineered 31 fourth-quarter comebacks and led 40 game-winning drives in his career. Perhaps none of those are better remembered than "The Drive," which was a 98-yard masterpiece led by Elway in the closing minutes of the fourth quarter of the AFC championship game. Elway led Denver down the field to tie the score against the Cleveland Browns in a game that Denver would win in overtime on a Rich Karlis field goal.

Elway was inducted into the Pro Football Hall of Fame in 2004 after being inducted into the College Football Hall of Fame in 2000.

Quarterback John Elway (#7) of the Denver Broncos turns to pitch to running back Gene Lang (#33) against the Cleveland Browns in the 1987 AFC championship game at Mile High Stadium on January 17, 1988, in Denver, CO. The Broncos defeated the Browns 38-33.

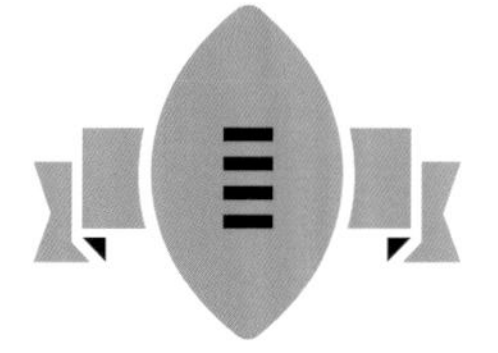

DOUG FLUTIE

BORN: OCTOBER 23, 1962, IN MANCHESTER, MARYLAND
HEIGHT: 5'9" (1.75 M) | WEIGHT: 177 LB (80 KG) | POSITION: QUARTERBACK
TEAM: BOSTON COLLEGE EAGLES
ACHIEVEMENTS: CONSENSUS ALL-AMERICAN (1984), HEISMAN TROPHY (1984)
INDUCTED INTO THE COLLEGE FOOTBALL HALL OF FAME IN 2007

If there was ever a poster child for thriving and succeeding in the challenging landscape of college football while being small in stature, Doug Flutie was it. At five feet, nine inches (1.75 m) tall, Flutie was anything but prototypical when it came to playing quarterback. While most quarterbacks are six foot three (1.9 m) and up with rocket arms and are fixtures in the pocket, Flutie was a scrambler, someone who could extend plays and make things happen with his legs. He surprised fans and opposing defenses on a weekly basis throughout his career.

Flutie played four years at Boston College from 1981 to 1984. Boston College was fairly successful in the Flutie era, posting three winning seasons in that span. Flutie will forever be remembered for a play in one game during his tenure at Boston College: trailing Miami (FL) 45-41 with six seconds to go on November 23, 1984, Flutie eluded the rush of Miami and flung the ball downfield. Receiver Gerard Phalen was on the other end of the Hail Mary, hauling it in and falling into the end zone as time expired. Boston College took an improbable 47-45 victory that was the icing on the cake in Flutie's Heisman Trophy-winning season.

Flutie was a starter from the instant he took the field at Boston College. The 1981 season was full of growing pains, both for the young quarterback and the Boston College team in general. Flutie completed 105 of 192 passes (54.7 percent completion rate) for 1,652 yards with 10 touchdown passes and eight interceptions. Boston College struggled to a 5-6 season under Flutie and coach Jack Bicknell, though they did win three of their final four games after losing five of their first seven.

Boston College improved as a team in 1982 even as Flutie regressed. Flutie threw the ball far more often, completing 162 of 347 passes (a meager 46.7 percent completion rate) for 2,749 yards with 13 touchdown passes against 20 interceptions. Still, Boston College improved from 5-6 to 8-3-1 on the year. Their record was good enough to earn a berth in the Tangerine Bowl against Auburn, where they were defeated 33-26. Boston College was 8-0 against unranked opponents, and 0-3-1 against ranked opponents, a 17-17 tie against then #16 Clemson the only high note in those contests.

Flutie's junior year of 1983 saw the Eagles begin flying high. Flutie bounced back from a down year his sophomore season as he completed 177 of 345 passes (51.3 percent

Doug Flutie (#7) of the Buffalo Bills passes the football during the AFC wild-card playoff game against the Miami Dolphins at Pro Player Stadium on January 2, 1999, in Miami Gardens, FL. The Dolphins defeated the Bills 24-17.

Riddell
7

completion rate) for 2,724 yards with 17 touchdown passes and 15 interceptions. He added 245 yards on the ground for the Eagles, who were bolstered by Troy Stradford at running back and the receiving skills of Brian Brennan, who caught 66 passes for over 1,100 yards and eight touchdowns. Boston College finished the year 9-3, including a win in the regular season finale over then 13th-ranked Alabama. The bowl game would once again be unkind, however, as Notre Dame turned back Boston College 19-18 in the Liberty Bowl. Flutie finished third in the Heisman Trophy race that year.

Flutie put it all together in 1984, his senior season. Bicknell put more faith in Flutie's ability to lead the offense and he delivered. Flutie completed 233 of 386 passes (60.4 percent completion rate) for 3,484 yards with 27 touchdown passes against just 11 interceptions. The Eagles were the top scoring team in the nation, averaging 37.4 points per game in 1984. Boston College finished 10-2 on the season, capped with a convincing 45-28 victory over Houston in the Cotton Bowl to end Flutie's college career. He won the Heisman Trophy in convincing fashion, outdistancing second-place finisher Keith Byars by 989 points, and was also named a consensus All-American selection.

Flutie was picked in the USFL territorial draft by the New Jersey Generals in 1985 and spent the year with that club. He was selected by the Los Angeles Rams in the 11th round of the 1985 NFL Draft but never played a down with the franchise. His rights were traded to the Chicago Bears for draft picks in 1986 after the demise of the USFL. Flutie would play in four games for the Bears before being dealt to the New England Patriots prior to the 1987 season. He would spend three years in New England before heading north of the border to play in the Canadian Football League. He played for the British Columbia Lions, the Calgary Stampeders, and the Toronto Argonauts in the CFL, winning the Most Outstanding Player Award a record six times.

Flutie returned to the NFL to play for the Buffalo Bills in 1998 and remained with the team through 2000. He spent the 2001 through 2004 seasons with the San Diego Chargers before closing his career with the Patriots again in 2005. Flutie completed 1,177 of 2,151 passes in the NFL (54.7 percent completion rate) for 14,715 yards with 86 touchdown passes against 68 interceptions. He posted a 38-28 record as a starting quarterback. His CFL numbers were tremendous: he completed 2,975 of 4,844 passes (61.4 percent completion rate) for 41,344 yards with 270 touchdown passes and 155 interceptions. He also ran for 4,660 yards and 66 touchdowns in the CFL.

Flutie was inducted to the College Football Hall of Fame in 2007, his first year of eligibility. Boston College also honored him for his heroics of the Hail Mary to Phelan by building a statue in 2008.

Quarterback Doug Flutie (#22) of the Boston College Eagles turns to hand the ball off against the Penn State Nittany Lions during an NCAA college football game October 29, 1983, at Alumni Stadium in Boston, MA.

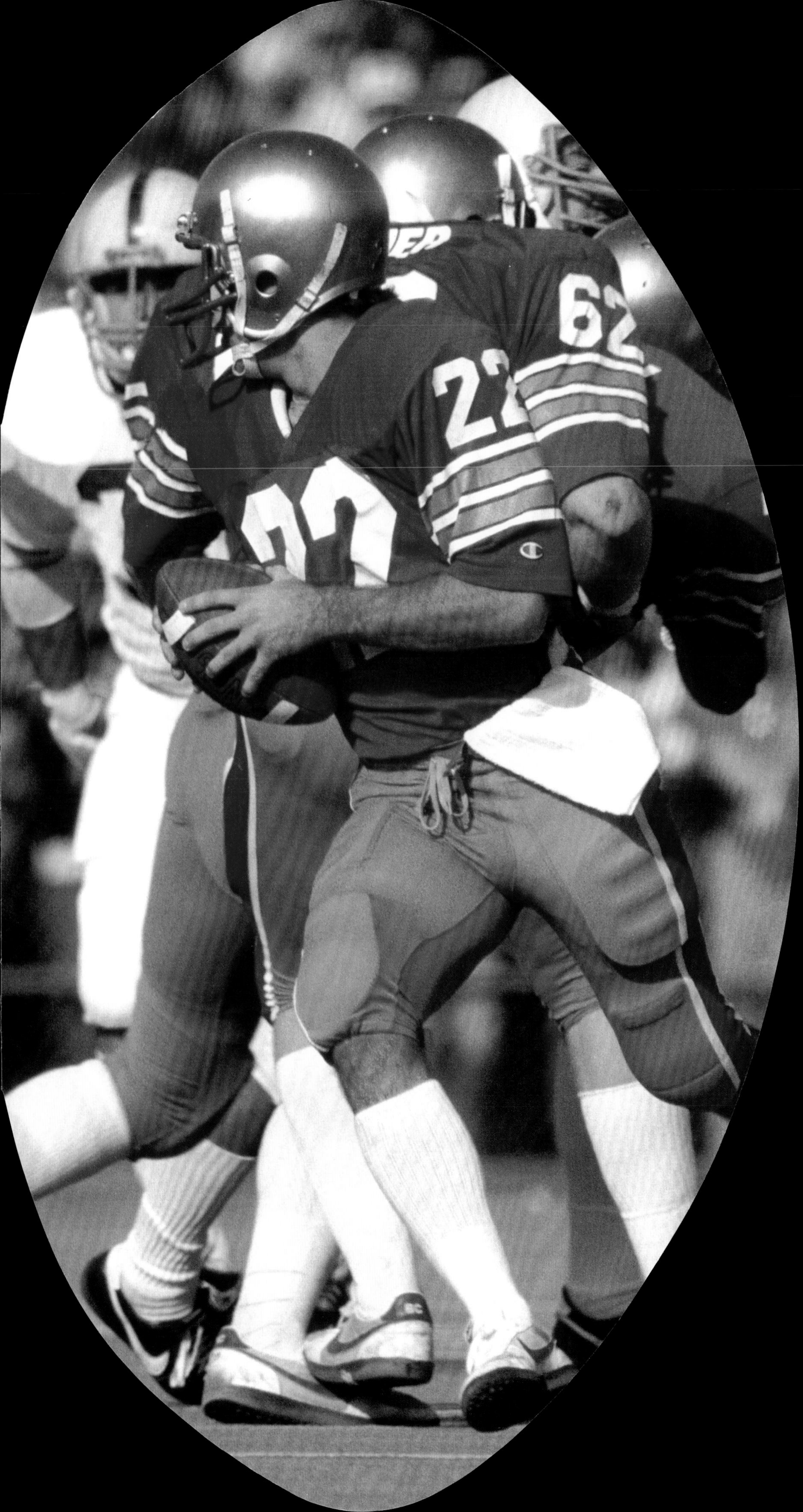
62
22

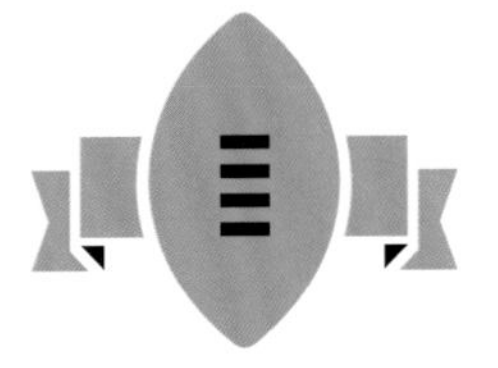

GEORGE GIPP

BORN: FEBRUARY 18, 1895, IN LAURIUM, MICHIGAN
HEIGHT: 6'1" (1.85 M) | WEIGHT: 180 LB (82 KG) | POSITION: HALFBACK
TEAM: UNIVERSITY OF NOTRE DAME FIGHTING IRISH
ACHIEVEMENTS: CONSENSUS ALL-AMERICAN (1920)
INDUCTED INTO THE COLLEGE FOOTBALL HALL OF FAME IN 1951

George Gipp may be immortalized in Hollywood films and invoked repeatedly by coaches during pep talks and pregame speeches, but he was an actual person as well. Gipp was a stalwart running back for Notre Dame for four years. When he left the school after that time, he was the Fighting Irish's leading rusher with 2,371 yards. That mark would end up standing for 58 more seasons, until 1978.

Gipp played in an era before bowl games, before polls by the media and coaches, and before football was saturating television and radio to the extent that it does today. There was no Heisman Trophy to be awarded, and most of the big rivalries that we're accustomed to today were in their infancy during his tenure at Notre Dame. Gipp played at the school from 1917 through 1920 and finished his career with 369 carries for 2,371 yards. He also completed 93 of 187 passes (49.7 percent completion rate) for 1,769 yards with eight touchdowns and 16 interceptions, punted 96 times, intercepted five passes on defense, and averaged 20.6 yards on 22 kickoff returns. Gipp was named a consensus All-American selection in 1920 and scored 156 points in a Notre Dame uniform (21 touchdowns, 27 extra points, one field goal).

Gipp began his career at Notre Dame in 1917 as a freshman. He ran the ball 63 times for 244 yards and completed three of eight throws for 40 yards with one touchdown pass and two interceptions. Gipp also punted 13 times and averaged 12.6 yards on eight punt returns. It was the only year in his college career that he failed to reach the end zone. Notre Dame finished the season 6-1-1, with the defense leading the way; the team allowed just nine points in the eight games. Notre Dame's only blemishes were a 7-0 defeat to Nebraska coming after a scoreless tie with Wisconsin. Army scored the other two points against Notre Dame that season in a 7-2 Irish victory. It was coach Jesse Harper's last season in South Bend. He left after the 1917 season with a 34-5-1 mark in five seasons at the school.

With Harper gone, the new coach at Notre Dame was Knute Rockne. Rockne was focused on continuing the tradition of excellence at the school and demanded the best from his players. Gipp did his best to respond to the challenge. He ran the ball 98 times for 541 yards and six scores, while completing 19 of 45 passes (42.2 percent completion rate) for 293 yards with one touchdown and one interception. Gipp punted 43 times,

George Gipp, running back of the Notre Dame University Fighting Irish, at Notre Dame Stadium in South Bend, IN.

kicked seven extra points, averaged 26.7 yards on three kickoff returns, and picked off a pass on defense. Notre Dame slipped, albeit slightly; with a shortened schedule, the Irish went 3-1-2 in 1918, tying Great Lakes Navy and Nebraska but dropping a 13-7 decision to Michigan State.

Gipp's junior season in 1919 was a success both for him and for Notre Dame as a team. He continued to improve his numbers from the year before, as he carried the ball 106 times for 729 yards and seven touchdowns. He completed 41 of 72 passes (56.9 percent completion rate) for 727 yards with three touchdown passes and four interceptions. Gipp also punted 12 times and kicked four extra points and one field goal. He averaged 20.8 yards on eight kickoff returns, ran back one punt for 12 yards, and intercepted three passes. Notre Dame rolled their way to a perfect 9-0 mark and the national championship.

The 1920 season would be Gipp's last at Notre Dame, and he did his best to make it memorable. He ran 102 times for 827 yards and eight touchdowns, while completing 30 of 62 passes (48.4 percent completion rate) for 709 yards with three touchdown passes and nine interceptions. He punted 28 times, kicked 16 extra points, averaged 18.9 yards on 11 kick returns, 15.1 yards on seven punt returns, and intercepted a pass on defense. Notre Dame again went 9-0, and was named the national champion by the Billingsley and Parke Davis reviews of those days. California and Princeton were the recognized national champions of the year.

Gipp's career was over at Notre Dame, and his life tragically came to an end shortly thereafter. He died of pneumonia on December 14, 1920, less than three weeks after the close of Notre Dame's season. He was 25 years of age. Gipp lives on even now, thanks to this statement he gave to Rockne before he died: "I gotta go, Rock," Gipp had said. "Someday, Rock, when the team is up against it, when things are going bad and breaks are beating the boys— tell them to go on in there with all they've got and win just one for The Gipper. I don't know where I'll be then, Rock, but I'll know about it, and I'll be happy."

Rockne used the "Win one for the Gipper" speech in 1928 when Notre Dame was trailing Army at halftime. The Irish, down 6-0 at the time, were invigorated and came from behind to claim a 12-6 victory. Gipp was inducted into the College Football Hall of Fame in 1951.

George Gipp, running back of the Notre Dame University Fighting Irish, at Notre Dame Stadium in South Bend, IN.

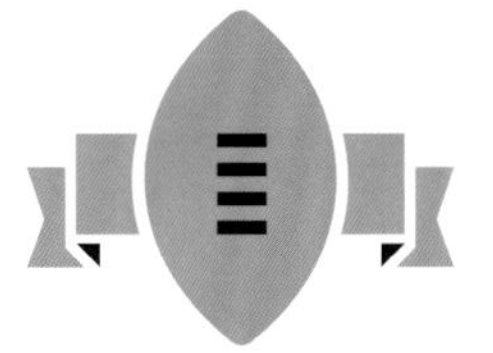

RED GRANGE

BORN: JUNE 13, 1903, IN FORKSVILLE, PENNSYLVANIA
HEIGHT: 6'0" (1.82 M) | WEIGHT: 175 LB (79 KG) | POSITION: HALFBACK
TEAM: UNIVERSITY OF ILLINOIS FIGHTING ILLINI
ACHIEVEMENTS: CONSENSUS ALL-AMERICAN (1923, 1924, 1925)
INDUCTED INTO THE COLLEGE FOOTBALL HALL OF FAME IN 1951

Red Grange lived up to the nickname "The Galloping Ghost" during his career at the University of Illinois. In his three years at the school, he scored 31 touchdowns in 20 games. Of the 20 games he played, he scored in 19 of those; the only team to keep him off the score sheet was Nebraska in a 1925 clash. Grange was dominant from the first time he stepped on a college field to the last game he played at Illinois. He scored three touchdowns in his very first college game, that against Nebraska in 1923.

Grange played at Illinois from 1923 to 1925, and was named a consensus All-American selection all three years. In his career, Grange ran the ball 388 times for 2,071 yards and 29 touchdowns. He added 14 receptions for 253 yards and two additional scores and completed 40 of 82 passes (48.8 percent completion rate) for 575 yards, three touchdown passes, and 11 interceptions. Of his 31 career touchdowns in college, 16 of them came from at least 20 yards, and nine of them covered at least 50 yards.

Grange originally planned to stick to basketball and track and field at Illinois, but changed his mind his sophomore year at the school. In seven games in 1923, Grange carried the ball 129 times for 723 yards and 11 touchdowns rushing, while adding 10 receptions for 178 yards and another touchdown. He also completed four of nine passes (44.4 percent) for 36 yards, returned one kickoff 7 yards and averaged 14.1 yards on 15 punt returns. Grange also punted once and intercepted three passes on defense, averaging 46.7 yards per return on those interceptions. Illinois finished the year a perfect 8-0 to claim the national championship. The team had five straight shutouts and allowed just 20 points all season.

Grange continued his assault on opposing defenses in 1924. He may be best known for his performance in the first game ever held at Memorial Stadium on October 18, 1924, when the Illini hosted Michigan. Grange ran the opening kickoff back 95 yards for a touchdown, then added scores of 67, 56, and 44 yards in the first quarter as Illinois bolted to a 27-0 lead. He would go on to run 11 yards for a fifth score in the second half and throw a 20-yard scoring pass for Illinois' sixth touchdown as they rolled the Wolverines 39-14 and ended Michigan's 20-game unbeaten run. Grange finished that contest with 402 total yards.

For the 1924 season, Grange had 113 carries for 743 yards and a dozen rushing

Portrait of Harold "Red" Grange (1903-1991), wearing a uniform and helmet, standing on a field holding a football, while playing for the University of Illinois.

HALL OF FAMER: RED GRANGE

touchdowns, along with two receptions for 40 yards. In addition, he completed 26 of 44 throws (59.1 percent completion rate) for 433 yards with two touchdown passes and four interceptions. Grange also averaged 34.5 yards on four kick returns and 7.5 yards on 11 punt returns on the season. He intercepted a pair of passes, picking up 24 yards on returns. Illinois finished the season with a record of 6-1-1, with a 20-7 loss to Minnesota in the next-to-last week of the season keeping them from an unbeaten mark.

Grange's senior year of 1925 was expected to be a continuation of his dominance in 1923 and 1924. Instead, Grange and the Illini struggled early on in the season. He had 146 carries for 605 yards and five touchdowns, while he caught two passes for 35 yards and another score. Grange struggled throwing the ball, completing just 10 of 29 throws (34.5 percent completion rate) for 106 yards with one touchdown and seven interceptions. He averaged 31 yards on 10 kick returns and 8.7 yards on 22 punt returns, while intercepting six passes on defense. Illinois finished 5-3, though they did win their last four games after losing three of their first four. Included in that was a surprising 24-2 upset of Penn.

Grange would go on to sign a contract with George Halas, the owner of the Chicago Bears, the day after the final college game of his career. Grange was given a salary and a cut of the gate receipts for the 19-game tour, which reportedly earned him $100,000. The tour helped save the New York Giants franchise thanks to a huge turnout at the Polo Grounds to see Grange play. He grew disgruntled with the Bears and eventually left the team after the 1925 season to form his own league, the American Football League. The AFL folded after one season and Grange's team was added to the NFL. Grange spent 1926 and 1927 with the New York Giants and suffered a knee injury while playing against the Bears. After missing the 1928 season, he returned to Chicago and played with the Bears from 1929 through 1934, and was part of two NFL championship teams in Chicago. He retired after the 1934 season with 21 rushing touchdowns and 10 receiving scores to his credit. Grange was inducted into the College Football Hall of Fame in 1951 and was a charter member of the Pro Football Hall of Fame in 1963. The University of Illinois retired Grange's number 77, one of only two numbers retired by the school; the other is fellow Hall of Famer Dick Butkus' number 50.

Portrait of the Chicago Bears' Red Grange at the start of his first professional game against the Cardinals.

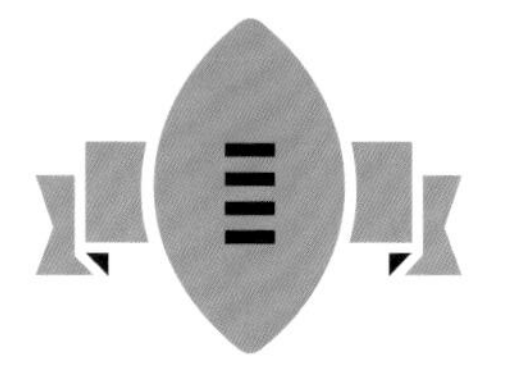

ARCHIE GRIFFIN

BORN: AUGUST 21, 1954, IN COLUMBUS, OHIO
HEIGHT: 5'9" (1.75 M) | WEIGHT: 182 LB (83 KG) | POSITION: RUNNING BACK
TEAM: OHIO STATE UNIVERSITY BUCKEYES
ACHIEVEMENTS: CONSENSUS ALL-AMERICAN (1974, 1975),
HEISMAN TROPHY (1974, 1975)
INDUCTED INTO THE COLLEGE FOOTBALL HALL OF FAME IN 1986

Archie Griffin was a terrific running back in college for Ohio State before having a successful professional career. Three times he broke the 1,000-yard plateau, and he is the only two-time winner of the Heisman Trophy in the history of the award since it was handed out beginning in 1936. Griffin was the linchpin of the Ohio State offense for the duration of his college career.

Griffin played four seasons at Ohio State from 1972 through 1975. He finished fifth in the Heisman voting in 1973 then won in his junior and senior seasons of 1974 and 1975. He also was a consensus All-American selection in both of those years. He amassed 5,167 yards on the ground to go along with 25 touchdowns. He won the Walter Camp Player of the Year Award in both 1974 and 1975 in addition to the Maxwell Award in 1975.

Griffin got to Columbus the first year that freshmen were allowed to play on the Ohio State football team. He won a starting job coming into the season as Ohio State ran out of the T-formation and proceeded to make an impact. He carried the ball 159 times and led the team with 867 yards on the ground while scoring three touchdowns. Ohio State won the Big Ten Conference and went to the Rose Bowl, where they were thumped 42-17 by USC for a disappointing end to the season. The Buckeyes finished 9-2 and were ranked ninth in the country in the final AP poll.

The 1973 season led to a change in the offensive strategy of Ohio State and an explosion in Griffin's numbers. Woody Hayes junked the T-formation for a more streamlined, modern I-formation offense that featured Griffin as the lead back. Griffin responded by delivering a tremendous season for the Buckeyes. He carried the ball 225 times for 1,428 yards and six touchdowns on the year, helping the Buckeyes to the Big Ten title again. Ohio State got revenge for their Rose Bowl loss to USC a year earlier, blasting the Trojans 42-21. The Buckeyes finished the year with a 10-0-1 record. The lone blemish on their mark was a 10-10 tie against Michigan in the season finale. The tie ended the eight-game win streak and cost them the #1 ranking in the country. Ohio State ended up second in the rankings at season's end.

The 1974 season continued Griffin's rise to stardom in college football. Griffin carried the ball 236 times for 1,620 yards and a dozen touchdowns. He won his first Heisman

Running back Archie Griffin (#45) of the Cincinnati Bengals carries the ball against the San Diego Chargers during a circa 1970s NFL game at Riverfront Stadium in Cincinnati, OH.

45

[illegible]ulating 483 first-place votes and 1,920 points to easily outdistance [illegible] finisher Anthony Davis of USC, who had 120 first-place votes and 819 [illegible] Ohio State was #1 in the country for seven weeks and won their first eight games [illegible] the year before a tough 16-13 loss to Michigan State in November. They rallied to win their final two games, including a 12-10 thriller over then third-ranked Michigan to claim another trip to the Rose Bowl. Griffin may have won the Heisman, but Davis and the Trojans got their revenge, winning the Rose Bowl 18-17 over the Buckeyes. Ohio State finished the year 10-2 and with the #4 ranking.

Instead of going pro, Griffin opted to come back for his senior season in 1975 and proceeded to deliver another outstanding year. He had his third straight 1,000-yard campaign as he carried the ball 245 times for 1,357 yards and four touchdowns. Griffin badly outdistanced the competition again in the Heisman, as he amassed 1,800 points to run away from second-place finisher Chuck Muncie, who finished with 730 points. Griffin was one of two 1,000-yard rushers for Ohio State in 1975 as Pete Johnson added 1,059 yards of his own on the ground. Ohio State rolled to an 11-0 regular season mark and another trip to the Rose Bowl. Once again, the Buckeyes were denied in Pasadena, as this time it was the UCLA Bruins that upended them by a count of 23-10. The loss snapped a nine-week run at #1; they finished #4 in the nation.

Griffin went on to the NFL after his college career was over, having been selected 24th overall in the first round by the Cincinnati Bengals. Griffin never captured his college success on the professional level, however, as he totaled just 2,808 yards and seven touchdowns in seven years in the NFL. He played sparingly for the Jacksonville Bulls of the USFL in 1985, carrying the ball 10 times for just 11 yards. For his accomplishments at the college level, Griffin was inducted into the College Football Hall of Fame in 1986.

Archie Griffin of the Cincinnati Bengals walking onto the field before an NFL football game against the Baltimore Colts at Memorial Stadium, September 19, 1976, in Baltimore, MD.

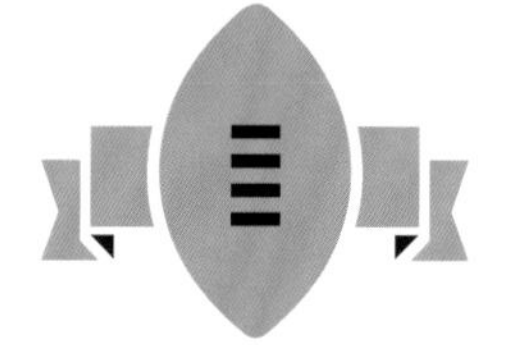

BO JACKSON

BORN: NOVEMBER 30, 1962, IN BESSEMER, ALABAMA
HEIGHT: 6'1" (1.85 M) | WEIGHT: 222 LB (101 KG) | POSITION: RUNNING BACK
TEAM: AUBURN UNIVERSITY TIGERS
ACHIEVEMENTS: CONSENSUS ALL-AMERICAN (1983, 1985),
HEISMAN TROPHY (1985)
INDUCTED INTO THE COLLEGE FOOTBALL HALL OF FAME IN 1998

Given the history of talented players to come out of Auburn University that went on to stardom in the National Football League, it's hard to come up with one that made more of a splash than Bo Jackson.

Jackson played four years at Auburn from 1982-85, and ran for 4,303 yards and 43 touchdowns as a member of the Tigers. Auburn was not well known for throwing the ball in those days, as they primarily focused on a run-oriented offense to grind out yards and maintain possession. In fact, the Tigers didn't throw for more than seven touchdowns in any of Jackson's four years at Auburn.

Still, none of that slowed Jackson down as he made his impact nonetheless. Jackson rushed for 829 yards and a team-high nine touchdowns as a freshman in 1982 as Auburn finished 9-3 with a Tangerine Bowl victory over Boston College. Auburn finished 14th in the final polls that season, and things were looking up for coach Pat Dye's Tigers with Jackson in the fold.

The 1983 season saw Jackson earn first-team All-American honors for the first time in his career. He took over the feature back role from Lionel James and lived up to the expectations, as he ran the ball 158 times for 1,213 yards and a dozen touchdowns. Jackson also made the most of the limited aerial attack that Auburn featured, catching 13 passes for 73 additional yards and two more scores. Auburn ended up 11-1 in 1983, winning their final 10 games, including a 9-7 victory over eighth-ranked Michigan in the Sugar Bowl. Auburn beat six ranked teams that year, including four teams ranked in the top eight during their final five games.

The 1984 season was disappointing for Jackson as he was injured for a good portion of it, leading to a precipitous decline in his numbers from 1983. Jackson carried the ball just 87 times for 475 yards and five touchdowns, which was good for just third on the team behind Brent Fullwood (628 yards) and Collis Campbell (511 yards) on the season. The season was disappointing for both Jackson and Auburn; after being the preseason #1 team in the nation, Auburn dropped their first two games and finished 9-4 on the season. Jackson was named the MVP of the Liberty Bowl, which Auburn won 21-15 over Arkansas. After finishing third in the polls in 1983, Auburn finished 14th in the nation

Bo Jackson (#34) of the Auburn Tigers on the field during a circa mid-1980s NCAA college football game in Auburn, AL.

34

in 1984.

Jackson's senior season of 1985 was Bo time. Jackson not only was named a first-team All-American for the second time in his collegiate career, he also walked away with the Heisman Trophy. He ran the ball 278 times for 1,786 yards and 17 touchdowns. Jackson and the Tigers were the #1 team in the land for three weeks, but a loss in late September to Tennessee knocked them from their lofty perch. Auburn would finish 8-4 and dropped their final two contests, including a 36-16 whipping by Texas A&M in the Cotton Bowl.

Jackson would run an NFL combined record 4.12-second 40-yard dash and was the first overall pick in the 1986 NFL Draft by the Tampa Bay Buccaneers, but he never played a down for the team. He instead decided to play major league baseball for the Kansas City Royals. When Jackson remained unsigned by the time the 1987 NFL Draft rolled around, the Buccaneers relinquished his rights and Jackson went back in the draft. The Los Angeles Raiders selected Jackson in the seventh round of the 1987 draft.

Jackson would play for the Raiders on a part-time basis from 1987-1990, joining the team after the baseball season had ended. He was the first player to ever be named an All-Star in two sports, being selected to the All-Star Game as a starter in baseball in 1989 and being named to the Pro Bowl in the NFL in 1990.

Jackson's NFL career came to an abrupt halt during the 1990 playoffs, when he sustained a serious hip injury in a win over the Cincinnati Bengals. He ended up having to have his hip replaced and never played football again, though he played baseball through the 1994 season.

There are few athletes who can excel at one sport. As an athlete who could thrive in multiple sports, Bo Jackson was part of an even rarer breed. Jackson was inducted into the College Football Hall of Fame in 1998.

Bo Jackson (#34) of the Los Angeles Raiders runs with the ball during an NFL football game against the Philadelphia Eagles on October 29, 1989, at Veterans Stadium in Philadelphia, PA.

34

...ELLY

...N, 14, 1960, IN PITTSBURGH, PENNSYLVANIA
...) | WEIGHT: 226 LB (103 KG) | POSITION: QUARTERBACK
...EAM: UNIVERSITY OF MIAMI (FL) HURRICANES
...IEVEMENTS: UNIVERSITY OF MIAMI (FL) HALL OF FAME (1992)
AND RING OF HONOR (2008)
INDUCTED INTO THE PRO FOOTBALL HALL OF FAME IN 2002

Sometimes decisions are made that completely alter the direction of an athlete's career. One of the biggest decisions that altered the arc of future Hall of Fame quarterback Jim Kelly's career was initially made not by the player himself, but by one of the most legendary coaches in the history of the sport.

Jim Kelly was born in Pittsburgh, Pennsylvania, and grew up in East Brady, a small town about 60 miles (97km) outside the Steel City. Kelly played football and basketball in high school, earning All-State honors as a senior as he threw for 3,915 yards plus 44 scoring passes. Being from Pennsylvania, Kelly wanted to go to Penn State and play for Joe Paterno; his dreams were shattered when Paterno said he wanted Kelly to convert to linebacker instead of quarterback. Penn State had already signed two All-State quarterbacks before getting to Kelly, which is why the offer of linebacker was made to him.

With his hopes of playing quarterback at Penn State gone, Kelly sought out other schools where he could play quarterback. He was recruited by Lou Saban, who was the coach of Miami (FL) in 1977 and 1978, and Kelly signed with the school after being guaranteed by Saban that he could play quarterback. He sat out the 1978 season as a redshirt freshman, giving him time to acclimate to the college game and learn the system.

By the time Kelly stepped on the field for the first time in a game situation, Saban was gone, having taken the head coaching position at Army. In Saban's stead was Howard Schnellenberger, who had been the offensive coordinator for the NFL's Miami Dolphins. Once Schnellenberger was hired, the school's trustees decided to keep the school as a member of Division I football instead of going down to Division I-AA. Former NFL quarterback Earl Morrall was hired on a volunteer basis to be quarterbacks coach, and the scene was set for Kelly to make his impact.

The 1979 season was Kelly's first with the Hurricanes and he began the year as the #2 quarterback on the depth chart behind Mike Rodrigue. Rodrigue was dismal and Miami (FL) struggled. They eked out a 6-0 win over Louisiana Tech and inexplicably were defeated 16-13 by Florida A&M. After a 25-15 loss to Syracuse to fall to 3-4,

Jim Kelly of the Buffalo Bills looks on, circa 1980s.

P.J.M.
12

Schnellenberger made the move to give Kelly his first career start. His opponent w none other than the school that turned him down in #19 Penn State. Kelly didn't know he was going to start until three hours before kickoff and, according to his own words, he promptly threw up when given the news. When the game took place, Kelly was ready to go as he hit 18 of 31 passes for 278 yards and three touchdowns to lead the Hurricanes to a 26-10 upset victory.

Miami (FL) finished the year 5-6, and Kelly completed 48 of 104 passes (46.2 percent completion rate) for 721 yards with five touchdowns and six interceptions, adding 53 yards and two scores on the ground. It was the start of a turnaround for the Hurricanes as they would begin to become relevant in the world of college football.

Kelly was the starter from the beginning of the 1980 season and led Miami to four straight victories to open the year, including a 10-9 win over then #9 Florida State on September 27. That victory propelled Miami to #13 in the rankings after being unranked the week before. Unfortunately, Miami dropped their next three as they were routed on the road by #7 Notre Dame, fell to Mississippi State by a field goal at home, and then were on the wrong side of a 27-12 score against #13 Penn State on the road. Suddenly, Miami was 4-3.

The rest of the season, Kelly and the Hurricanes were firing on all cylinders. They won their last five contests, including a 31-7 pasting of #18 Florida on the road, and earned a Peach Bowl berth against Virginia Tech. In that contest, Kelly completed 11 of 22 passes for 179 yards with a touchdown and an interception. He was named Offensive MVP for his efforts in the contest as Miami defeated the Hokies 20-10 to finish the year 9-3 and #18 in the country. Kelly finished the season 109 of 206 passing (52.9 percent completion rate) for 1,519 yards with 11 touchdowns against seven interceptions while adding 36 yards plus a pair of touchdowns on the ground. His 11 passing scores tied the school record for passing touchdowns in a season.

As solid as he was in 1980, Kelly improved in 1981 and the Hurricanes were a better team around him as well. Kelly led the team to an upset win over #17 Florida, 21-20, in the season opener, but after starting 2-0, Miami lost two of their next three as they fell 14-7 on the road to #4 Texas and 14-10 to #16 Mississippi State, also on the road. It proved to be the final defeat the Hurricanes took that season as things clicked into place after that.

Miami went on to win their final six games of the year, including a 17-14 victory over #1 Penn State on October 31 at the Orange Bowl. Kelly hit 13 of 25 passes for 220 yards plus an 80-yard touchdown pass to Larry Brodsky to help the Hurricanes to the upset win; Miami followed that with a 27-19 road win over #14 Florida State a week later. The

Quarterback Jim Kelly of the Buffalo Bills drops back to pass against the New York Jets during an NFL football game r 15, 1991, at Giants Stadium in East Rutherford, NJ.

Hurricanes closed the year with a 37-15 trouncing of Notre Dame to end up 9-2 though they didn't make a bowl game. Kelly completed 168 of 285 passes (58.9 percent) for 2,403 yards with a school record 14 touchdown passes and 14 interceptions plus three scores on the ground as the Hurricanes finished #8 in the final rankings.

Kelly was a potential Heisman Trophy candidate in his senior year in 1982 but the winds of fate didn't blow his way. He suffered a complete shoulder separation against Virginia Tech in the third week of the season that required reconstructive surgery and was finished for the year. Kelly finished the year hitting 51 of 81 passes (63 percent completion rate) for 585 yards with three touchdowns and one interception. Miami struggled a bit without him, finishing 7-4 as future Georgia head coach Mark Richt struggled to run the offense.

Kelly finished his collegiate career completing 406 of 646 passes for 5,228 yards with 33 touchdown passes and 28 interceptions. While his numbers weren't overwhelming compared to today's standards, the fact that the passing game wasn't as prevalent in that era shows how much the game has changed. Kelly was inducted into the Miami (FL) Hall of Fame in 1992 and into the school's Ring of Honor in 2008.

Perhaps more important than his numbers as a college quarterback is the pipeline that Kelly helped create. Miami (FL) was a program on its deathbed before he played for the school. After he played, the Hurricanes attracted a string of solid to spectacular quarterbacks, and Bernie Kosar, Vinny Testaverde, Steve Walsh, Craig Erickson, Gino Torretta, and Ken Dorsey all followed him at the school that was later dubbed "Quarterback U." All but Kosar won a national title while at the school and Testaverde and Torretta won the Heisman Trophy.

Kelly was drafted with the 14th overall pick in the quarterback-loaded 1983 NFL Draft by the Buffalo Bills but he didn't play for the team until 1986, as he spent two seasons playing with the Houston Gamblers of the USFL. During that time, he completed 730 of 1,154 passes (63.3 percent completion rate) for 9,842 yards with 83 touchdowns and 45 interceptions. When the USFL folded, Kelly worked out a five-year deal worth $7.5 million to play for the Bills beginning in 1986.

He spent his entire NFL career with the Bills, leading Buffalo to four straight Super Bowls between 1990 and 1993. Kelly retired after the 1996 season after completing 2,874 of 4,779 passes (60.1 percent completion rate) for 35,467 yards with 237 touchdown passes and 175 interceptions. He added 1,049 yards and seven touchdowns on the ground. For his efforts, Kelly's number was retired by the Bills in 2001 and he was inducted into the Pro Football Hall of Fame in 2002.

Buffalo Bills quaterback Jim Kelly looks downfield to pass, against the Miami Dolphins, Buffalo, NY, 1996.

…AGURSKI

…, 1908, IN RAINY RIVER, ONTARIO, CANADA
…6 M) | WEIGHT: 217 LB (98 KG) | POSITION: TACKLE
…UNIVERSITY OF MINNESOTA GOLDEN GOPHERS
…ACHIEVEMENTS: CONSENSUS ALL-AMERICAN (1929)
…NDUCTED INTO THE COLLEGE FOOTBALL HALL OF FAME IN 1951

Bronko Nagurski was a proverbial battering ram of a football player, capable of and seemingly bent on wiping out anyone and anything that was in his path. Unlike most athletes today who are scouted and signed years before they actually get to college, Nagurski was signed after University of Minnesota coach Clarence Spears drove up to International Falls, Minnesota. He discovered Nagurski plowing a field on his family's farm and convinced him to attend college. The rest, as they say, is history.

Nagurski made his impact during practice, showing Spears and the rest of the Golden Gophers that he was ready for business. In the "Nutcracker" drill, where a defensive player has to deal with two blockers in an effort to take down a ball carrier, Nagurski split the two blockers and steamrolled the running back. Spears, caught by surprise, sent out two more blockers and a ball carrier, only to see Nagurski produce the same result. It wasn't long until Nagurski was doing the same thing to opposing teams. He was a force to be reckoned with in his three years at the school from 1927 to 1929.

Nagurski's statistics pale in comparison to most players, mainly due to the incompleteness of most statistics kept during the era and the difference in the game from then to the current time. Nagurski didn't play a skill position like quarterback or running back in his first year at Minnesota, focusing instead on playing tackle. He helped lead an offense that rushed for over 2,500 yards as Minnesota went 6-0-2 on the season. Ties with Indiana and Notre Dame were the only thing that prevented the Golden Gophers from going 8-0.

The 1928 campaign had Nagurski playing on both sides of the ball: he was a running back, normally deployed as a fullback on offense, and played on the defensive line. He carried the ball 74 times for 298 yards and scored three touchdowns on offense for the Golden Gophers. His toughness was shown in a game against Wisconsin that year, when nursing a broken rib that was protected by a corset, Nagurski recovered a Badger fumble deep in Wisconsin territory. He then proceeded to carry the ball six straight times to score a touchdown. He later would intercept a pass in the game to preserve Minnesota's 6-0 win in the season finale. Minnesota finished the year 6-2-0, with a pair of one-point losses to Iowa and Northwestern costing them a perfect mark.

The 1929 season was Nagurski's last with the Golden Gophers. He led the nation with

Canadian-born NFL football player Bronislaw "Bronko" Nagurski (1908-1990) runs with the football inside a stadium, 1930s.

737 yards on the ground and was a consensus All-American selection at fullback. He also drew quite a few votes for an All-American slot at defensive tackle, despite not playing that position full time. Well-respected writer Grantland Rice put Nagurski at both spots in his All-American team in 1929. The Golden Gophers would go 6-2 again in 1929, giving them a mark of 18-4-2 in Nagurski's three years at the school. Again, the losses were close: a two-point defeat at Iowa was followed by a one-point loss to Michigan. The four losses Minnesota suffered while Nagurski was there were by a combined five points.

Nagurski turned pro following his college career and spent 1930 through 1937 Chicago Bears before returning for one final season in 1943, as teams were ue to World War II. Nagurski was known for the jump pass, where he into the line after taking a handoff, and then jump back while jump pass to Red Grange helped the Bears win the 1932 is pro career with 4,031 yards rushing along with 25 passes for 134 yards and completed 32 of 77 sses and nine interceptions.

the 1937 season, Nagurski walked stling, where he was wildly World Champion in 1939 ski would win the ndor Szabo

BARRY SANDERS

BORN: JULY 16, 1968, IN WICHITA, KANSAS
HEIGHT: 5'8" (1.73 M) | WEIGHT: 197 LB (89 KG) | POSITION: RUNNING BACK
TEAM: OKLAHOMA STATE UNIVERSITY COWBOYS
ACHIEVEMENTS: CONSENSUS ALL-AMERICAN (1988), HEISMAN TROPHY (1988)
INDUCTED INTO THE COLLEGE FOOTBALL HALL OF FAME IN 2003

Barry Sanders was as dynamic a running back as college football has seen in the past quarter century, if not longer. He was explosive, elusive, versatile, and wildly effective. The only thing that kept Sanders' numbers down his first two seasons at Oklahoma State was the fact that he played behind another top-flight running back and future NFL Hall of Fame inductee in Thurman Thomas.

Sanders played three seasons at Oklahoma State from 1986 through 1988. He was Thomas' backup in 1986 and 1987, but when Thomas entered the NFL Draft and was taken by the Buffalo Bills in 1988, Sanders exploded with a season for the ages. His winning of the Heisman Trophy and selection as a consensus All-American pick in 1988 was a surprise to no one. After his tremendous junior season, Sanders declared for the NFL Draft.

The 1986 campaign was Sanders' first in Stillwater and Oklahoma State. He was clearly number two in the pecking order as far as carrying the ball, as Thomas got the majority of the work. While Thomas had 173 carries for 741 yards and four touchdowns, Sanders got the ball 73 times for 325 yards and three scores as a freshman. He also made his impact on special teams, returning punts and kicks. Sanders averaged 23.7 yards per kick return on seven attempts and 5.4 yards per return on eight punts. Oklahoma State finished 6-5 in 1986, closing the year with three straight victories.

The 1987 season saw another year of Sanders backing up Thomas. Thomas had a huge campaign, carrying 250 times for 1,613 yards and 18 touchdowns on the ground. There was still a fair amount of work for Sanders in the backfield as well, and he carried the ball 105 times for 603 yards and eight touchdowns. He also added four receptions for an additional 59 yards and a score, averaged 31.6 yards on 14 kick returns and 16.3 yards on 15 punt returns. Sanders was stifled in the Sun Bowl, carrying six times for just 19 yards in the Cowboys' 35-33 victory over the West Virginia Mountaineers. The bowl victory helped Oklahoma State finish the season with a mark of 10-2 and they were the 11th-ranked team in the nation.

The 1988 season left the backfield all to Sanders with the departure of Thurman Thomas, and Sanders delivered in a huge fashion. Sanders rushed for 2,628 yards on 344 carries and scored an astounding 37 touchdowns rushing. He added an additional

Barry Sanders of the Detroit Lions carries the ball against the Chicago Bears during an NFL football game November 3, 1991, at Soldier Field in Chicago, IL.

JRT

o yards and two more touchdowns, giving him an NCAA record 39 n the season. Despite the heavy workload running the ball, Sanders still kicks and averaged 20 yards per return on 21 kick returns and 10.6 yards per t return on nine run backs. Sanders wasn't done though: he ran for 222 yards and five more touchdowns in the Holiday Bowl against Wyoming, which Oklahoma State won in a rout 62-14. Oklahoma State was the highest scoring team in the nation in 1988, averaging 48.7 points per game. They were held to less than 41 points just once in 12 games, in a 31-28 loss to Oklahoma. The team finished 10-2 and with the #11 ranking for the second season in a row.

With the Heisman Trophy and an All-American selection firmly in his back pocket, Sanders declared for the NFL Draft after his junior season. He was drafted with the third overall pick by the Detroit Lions in the 1989 NFL Draft. He was named the NFL Offensive Rookie of the Year, went to the Pro Bowl and was an All-Pro selection that season as well. Sanders played his entire career with the Lions, retiring after the 1998 season with 15,269 yards rushing and 109 touchdowns. He was named to the Pro Bowl 10 times and was an All-Pro selection 10 times. During his career, Sanders also led the league in rushing four times, and was named the NFL MVP in 1997. He was inducted to the Pro Football Hall of Fame in 2004 and the College Football Hall of Fame in 2003. The Lions also retired his number 20 following the conclusion of his career.

Barry Sanders carries the ball against the Tampa Bay Buccaneers, October 2, 1994, during an NFL football game at Tampa Stadium in Tampa Bay, FL.

20

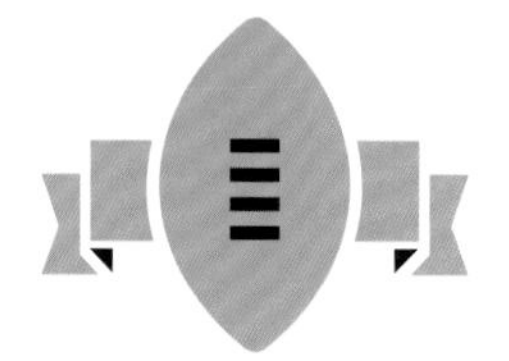

ROGER STAUBACH

BORN: FEBRUARY 5, 1942, IN CINCINNATI, OHIO
HEIGHT: 6'3" (1.91 M) | WEIGHT: 190 LB (86 KG) | POSITION: QUARTERBACK
TEAM: UNITED STATES NAVAL ACADEMY NAVY MIDSHIPMEN
ACHIEVEMENTS: CONSENSUS ALL-AMERICAN (1963), HEISMAN TROPHY (1963)
INDUCTED INTO THE COLLEGE FOOTBALL HALL OF FAME IN 1981

Roger Staubach was a rare breed in many ways. He was one of the few players of his era to make a major impact in the National Football League after playing collegiately at a military academy. He played college football at Navy, spending three years as the quarterback of the offense for the Midshipmen. He was drafted in the 1964 NFL Draft but due to military commitments, he did not suit up in the NFL until 1969.

The Naval Academy—much like its brethren Army, playing at West Point, and the Air Force Academy— tends to have a run-oriented offense, which limits a team's passing attack. It seemed a bit of an odd fit with Staubach, who was fully capable of throwing the ball, going to an offense where the pass was eschewed for the option. He played football for one year at the New Mexico Military Institute before getting to Navy.

Staubach made his debut as a member of the Midshipmen in a 21-0 defeat at the hands of the Minnesota Golden Gophers on October 6, 1962. He was 0-for-2 and was sacked twice in relief of starting quarterback Ron Klemick. The Minnesota defense featured future NFL Hall of Famers Carl Eller and Bobby Bell. Staubach finished the season completing 66 of 98 throws (67.3 percent completion rate) for 966 yards, seven touchdowns, and just three interceptions. He even led the Midshipmen to a stunning 34-14 thumping of Army in the annual game between the service academies. Navy finished the year with a mark of 5-5.

The 1963 season was a banner year for Staubach and Navy. Staubach claimed the Heisman Trophy and the Maxwell Award, beating out Billy Lothridge of Georgia Tech by a wide margin. Staubach completed 107 of 161 passes (66.5 percent completion rate) for 1,474 yards, seven touchdown passes, and six interceptions. He added 418 yards on the ground on 156 carries. Navy rolled to a 9-1 mark in the regular season, with their lone loss a four-point setback at the hands of SMU. Included in the run were wins over then #3 Pittsburgh, Army, and Notre Dame. The victory over the Fighting Irish was important; Navy would not beat the Fighting Irish again until 2007. Playing top-ranked Texas in the Cotton Bowl for the national title, Navy came up short, falling 28-6. They finished second in the final poll of the season. Staubach was a consensus All-American selection for his performance.

A passing portrait of Navy quarterback Roger Staubach, September 23, 1963.

HALL OF FAMER: ROGER STAUBACH

The 1964 season was Staubach's senior year at Navy, and he once again was more than capable of leading the Midshipmen. With less talent around him than in the previous two years, his numbers dropped. He completed 119 of 204 passes (58.3 percent completion rate) for 1,131 yards and four touchdowns against 10 interceptions. Staubach couldn't generate any yards on the ground, as he ended up with a net total of minus-1 yard on the season. The Midshipmen scuffled to a record of 3-6-1, going 0-5-1 in a six-game stretch and culminating with a loss to Army to end their season.

Staubach was drafted by the Dallas Cowboys in the 10th round of the 1964 NFL Draft, and also by the Kansas City Chiefs in the 16th round of the 1964 AFL Draft. He had to serve his military commitment before he could play in the NFL. Rather than be stationed stateside, Staubach served a one-year tour in Vietnam as a supply corps officer then spent the remainder of his time in the United States. He played on several barnstorming-type teams as he prepared to transition from soldier to civilian, and in his case, professional athlete.

Staubach was 27 years old when he made his NFL debut as a rookie with the Dallas Cowboys in 1969. He played 11 seasons in the NFL, all with Dallas. During that time, he led the Cowboys to five Super Bowl appearances and a pair of Super Bowl victories. Staubach was the Super Bowl MVP in Dallas' 24-3 win over the Miami Dolphins in Super Bowl VI. He was named to the Pro Bowl on six occasions and led the league in passer rating four times. He retired after the 1979 season and was inducted into the Pro Football Hall of Fame in 1985. Staubach was also enshrined in the College Football Hall of Fame in 1981, and had his number retired by the Naval Academy at graduation.

ABOVE: *Navy quarterback Roger Staubach gets sacked in a 13-6 loss to USC Trojans on November 17, 1962, at Los Angeles Memorial Coliseum in Los Angeles, CA.*
RIGHT: *Quarterback Roger Staubach (#12) of the Dallas Cowboys drops back to pass during a game on September 19, 1971, against the Buffalo Bills at War Memorial Stadium in Buffalo, NY.*

JIM THORPE

BORN: MAY 28, 1888, IN POTTAWATOMIE COUNTY, OKLAHOMA
HEIGHT: 6'1" (1.85 M) | WEIGHT: 185 LB (84 KG) | POSITION: HALFBACK
TEAM: CARLISLE INDIAN INDUSTRIAL SCHOOL INDIANS
ACHIEVEMENTS: CONSENSUS ALL-AMERICAN (1911, 1912)
INDUCTED INTO THE COLLEGE FOOTBALL HALL OF FAME IN 1951

Jim Thorpe was more than just a football player; he was a tremendous all-around athlete. In his lifetime, Thorpe played football on a collegiate and professional level, while also playing baseball and basketball professionally. He won gold medals in both the pentathlon and decathlon at the 1912 Olympics before having them taken away for violating the amateur status rule. He had played semi-pro baseball for two years prior to the Olympics. In 1983, thirty years after he died, the International Olympic Committee voted to restore Thorpe's medals.

Thorpe played four years at Carlisle Indian Industrial School under the watchful eye of legendary coach Pop Warner. Thorpe played in 1907 and 1908, and then worked on a farm for a couple of years after the death of his father before returning to the school in 1911 and 1912. He was a consensus All-American selection in both 1911 and 1912, making a major impact in the world of football while the sport was still in its relative infancy.

Thorpe began his college career in 1907 with Carlisle. His appearances were sparing, as Pop Warner was still reticent to put his best athlete on the field and risk injury. Thorpe had just 16 carries for 67 yards, though he did find the end zone six times. He was held in check, averaging just 3.3 yards on three punt returns. Carlisle finished the year with a 10-1 mark, the only loss a 16-0 blanking at the hands of Princeton. Along the way, Carlisle blasted Susquehanna 91-0 and also turned away Harvard, Syracuse, Minnesota, and Pennsylvania.

Thorpe got more of an opportunity to showcase his abilities in 1908. During that season, he carried the ball 113 times for 781 yards and four touchdowns. He also managed to complete 8 of 13 passes (61.5 percent completion rate) for 212 yards with a touchdown pass. Thorpe was extremely proficient in the kicking game. He punted the ball 49 times, kicked 13 extra points and six field goals, and was effective in the return game as well. Thorpe averaged 25 yards on two kick returns and 10.3 yards on 14 punt returns on the season. Carlisle went 10-2-1 on the season, their losses coming to Harvard and Minnesota, two teams they had upended the year before.

With the death of his father, Thorpe left school and did not return until 1911. That was when the rest of the nation got their first real look at what Thorpe could do as an athlete. He carried the ball 113 times for 899 yards and 14 touchdowns, while

ath portrait of Jim Thorpe posing in a football uniform on a field.

completing one of four throws for 15 yards and two interceptions. Thorpe punted the ball 39 times, kicked 19 extra points, and added seven field goals on the season. He averaged 17 yards on two kick returns, 12 yards on nine punt returns, and intercepted his first career pass on defense. Thorpe was a consensus All-American for the first time in his career in 1911. Carlisle finished the season with a mark of 11-1, with a one-point loss to Syracuse in mid-November being the team's only defeat.

Thorpe was dominant in his final year at Carlisle. He carried the ball 191 times for a staggering 1,869 yards and found the end zone 29 times. He added two catches for 40 yards, and completed 8 of 18 throws (44.4 percent completion rate) for 103 yards and an interception. Thorpe had an interception that he returned 95 yards, and averaged 20.4 yards on nine kick returns and 10 yards on 26 punt returns. He also punted the ball 45 times and kicked 38 extra points and four field goals. Thorpe had a 92-yard touchdown run called back on a penalty in Carlisle's game against Army, but on the next play he took the handoff and went 97 yards for a score. Carlisle finished the season with a 12-1-1 mark. A scoreless tie against Washington & Jefferson and a seven-point defeat to Penn late in the season kept them from a perfect record.

After his college career was over, Thorpe played professional baseball for the New York Giants, Cincinnati Reds, and Boston Braves before retiring in 1919 with a .252 career average, seven home runs, and 82 runs batted in. He would play for several teams in the APFA, which later became the NFL. His NFL career numbers included 52 games, six touchdowns rushing, three extra points, and four field goals. Thorpe was named a first-team All-Pro in 1923 and was inducted into the Pro Football Hall of Fame in the charter class of 1963. He also was inducted into the College Hall of Fame in 1951.

ABOVE: *Hall of Fame football player and all-around athlete, Jim Thorpe, 1925.*
RIGHT: *Jim Thorpe wearing a Canton Bulldogs football jersey.*

DOAK WALKER

BORN: JANUARY 1, 1927, IN DALLAS, TEXAS
HEIGHT: 5'11" (1.80 M) | WEIGHT: 170 LB (77 KG) | POSITION: HALFBACK
TEAM: SOUTHERN METHODIST UNIVERSITY MUSTANGS
ACHIEVEMENTS: CONSENSUS ALL-AMERICAN (1947, 1948, 1949), HEISMAN TROPHY (1948)
INDUCTED INTO THE COLLEGE FOOTBALL HALL OF FAME IN 1959

Doak Walker was the epitome of a do-it-all player during his college career at Southern Methodist University. Walker threw the ball as a quarterback, ran like a halfback, kicked extra points and field goals, returned kicks, and even played defense. Even more impressive than his versatility was the fact that he performed all these tasks with a high degree of skill and ability.

Walker played four seasons at Southern Methodist, covering 1945 and 1947 through 1949. He did not play in 1946 as he was serving in the United States Army. Walker was a consensus All-American selection his final three years of college and finished in the top three of the Heisman voting in each of those years. He finished third in 1947 when he won the Maxwell Award, won the Heisman in 1948, and finished third again in 1949. His contributions to SMU football and to the sport in general around the Dallas, Texas, area led to the Cotton Bowl being known as "The House that Doak Built."

Walker's freshman season at SMU saw him play sparingly. He carried the ball 58 times for 289 yards while adding a pair of receptions for 32 yards. Walker also completed 38 of 65 passes (58.5 percent completion rate) for 387 yards with one touchdown pass and four interceptions, punted 11 times, averaged 23 yards on five kickoff returns, and 15.9 yards on 15 punt returns. If that wasn't enough, he added a pair of interceptions on defense as well. SMU finished the year 5-6 and out of bowl contention. The 1946 season saw Walker in the Army, so he was out of action as the school went 4-5-1 in his absence.

After the year off, Walker returned for his sophomore season in 1947 and picked up where he had left off previously. He led SMU in rushing with 653 yards on 163 carries, added eight receptions for 132 yards, and completed 30 of 52 passes (57.7 percent completion rate) for 344 yards with two touchdown passes and three interceptions. Walker also kicked 18 extra points and one field goal, while punting 11 times and scoring 11 touchdowns. He averaged 38.7 yards per return on 10 kickoffs, 12.9 yards per return on 20 punts, and he intercepted two passes on defense. He finished third in the Heisman Trophy voting behind John Lujack of Notre Dame and Bob Chappius of Michigan. SMU won their first nine regular season games before tying TCU in the regular season finale. They closed the year with a 13-13 tie against Penn State in the Cotton Bowl to finish with a 9-0-2 mark and a #3

Running back Doak Walker (#37) of the Southern Methodist University Mustangs circa 1949 in Dallas, TX.

37

...s.

...Walker returned for his junior season in 1948 intent on improving himself. ...he ball 109 times for 537 yards, added 14 receptions for 264 additional yards ...ree touchdowns, and completed 26 of 47 passes (55.3 percent completion rate) for ...18 yards, six touchdowns, and five interceptions. He added eight touchdowns rushing and 22 extra points to account for 88 points on the season. In addition, Walker averaged 32.2 yards on five kick returns, 16.9 yards on 10 punt returns, and intercepted three passes on defense. SMU went 8-1-1 in the regular season, with an early-season defeat to Missouri and another tie in the season finale with TCU the only blemishes on their record. They returned to the Cotton Bowl, where they defeated 10th-ranked Oregon 21-13 to finish 9-1-1 and 10th in the nation in the final polls. Walker won the Heisman Trophy for his efforts.

Walker continued his do-it-all mentality in his senior year of 1949. SMU wasn't as talented a program, so yards were tougher to come by for the star running back. He carried the ball 130 times for 449 yards and added three receptions for 26 yards and a touchdown. He completed 34 of 58 passes (58.6 percent completion rate) for 605 yards, five touchdown passes, and six interceptions, punted 23 times, kicked 17 extra points, averaged 16.8 yards on six kick returns, 17.2 yards on five punt returns, and intercepted one pass on defense. SMU was not nearly as successful as they had been in 1947 and 1948, however. After starting out 5-1-1 through their first seven games, SMU dropped their final three contests, including a seven-point loss to top-ranked Notre Dame in the season finale to finish 5-4-1. Walker finished third in the Heisman Trophy voting, trailing Leon Hart of Notre Dame and Charlie Justice of North Carolina.

His college career complete, Walker turned professional. He was selected by the New York Bulldogs with the third overall pick in the 1949 NFL Draft, but he never played for the team. The Bulldogs folded after the 1951 NFL season. Walker instead ended up with the Detroit Lions, where he played his entire six-year NFL career. He made the decision to retire after the 1955 season, having won two NFL championships, five Pro Bowl selections, and the 1950 NFL Rookie of the Year Award.

Walker finished his pro career with 1,520 yards rushing on 309 carries and a dozen touchdowns. He also caught 152 passes for 2,539 yards and 21 additional touchdowns. Walker booted 49 of 87 field goal attempts, punted 50 times for a 39.1-yard average, and converted 183 of 191 extra point attempts in his career. He averaged 15.8 yards on 18 punt returns, including one for a touchdown, and 25.5 yards per return on 38 kickoffs. Walker was inducted into the College Football Hall of Fame in 1959 and the Pro Football Hall of Fame in 1986.

Running back Doak Walker (#37) of the Detroit Lions circa 1951 in Detroit, MI. Walker played for the Lions from 1950-55.

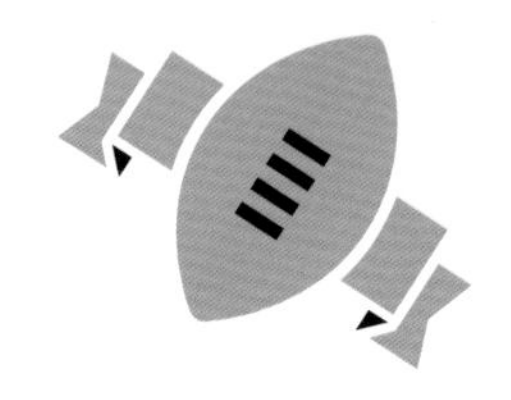

HERSCHEL WALKER

BORN: MARCH 3, 1962, IN WRIGHTSVILLE, GEORGIA
HEIGHT: 6'1" (1.85 M) | WEIGHT: 222 LB (101 KG) | POSITION: RUNNING BACK
TEAM: UNIVERSITY OF GEORGIA BULLDOGS
ACHIEVEMENTS: CONSENSUS ALL-AMERICAN (1980, 1981, 1982), HEISMAN TROPHY (1982)
INDUCTED INTO THE COLLEGE FOOTBALL HALL OF FAME IN 1999

Herschel Walker almost single-handedly returned the Georgia Bulldogs to prominence in college football during his career at the school. The Bulldogs won just one SEC title from 1968 to 1979, but when Walker was a part of the team from 1980 through 1982, they won each of those three years. Walker won the Heisman Trophy in 1982, just the second Bulldog ever to win the award and the first since Frank Sinkwich in 1942. No other Georgia player since has claimed the coveted award.

In his three-year tenure at Georgia, Walker helped lead the Bulldogs to an overall mark of 33-3 and a perfect 18-0 record within the Southeastern Conference. Included in that was a perfect 12-0 mark in 1980, capped by a Sugar Bowl win over Notre Dame to give Georgia the national championship. Walker finished his career with 5,259 yards and 49 rushing touchdowns, while adding 26 receptions for an additional 243 yards and three scores. He was a consensus All-American selection all three years at Georgia and finished in the top three of the Heisman voting each year: third in 1980, second in 1981, and he won the award in 1982.

Walker made an impact from the moment he stepped onto the football field at Georgia. The Bulldogs' offense revolved around his ability to make things happen with the ball. Walker carried the ball 274 times for 1,616 yards and 15 touchdowns. That yardage total set the NCAA record for rushing yards by a freshman. The Bulldogs went undefeated in the regular season, capturing the #1 ranking in the nation in early November and holding onto it through the rest of the regular season. Their 17-10 victory over Notre Dame in the Sugar Bowl gave Georgia the national championship. Walker finished third in the Heisman voting, behind only George Rogers of South Carolina and Hugh Green of Pittsburgh.

The 1981 season was another stellar year for Walker and Georgia. The Bulldogs roared through the SEC again with a perfect 6-0 mark. An early-season loss to Clemson dashed Georgia's hopes of a second consecutive unbeaten season, but they rebounded with eight consecutive victories to close the regular season with a 10-1 mark and a #2 ranking in the nation. Walker was a key cog in that run, carrying the ball 385 times for 1,891 yards and 18 touchdowns while catching 14 passes for 84 yards and

Running back Herschel Walker (#34) of the Philadelphia Eagles carries the ball against the Dallas Cowboys during an NFL football game December 4, 1994, at Veterans Stadium in Philadelphia, PA.

34
34

two touchdowns. The Bulldogs headed to the Sugar Bowl again but were upended by 10th-ranked Pittsburgh, who turned Georgia away by a score of 24-20. Walker finished second in the Heisman voting in 1981, trailing only USC running back Marcus Allen.

The 1982 season was Walker's junior year, and ultimately his last in college. Walker continued to be a dominant force in the Georgia offense, as he carried the ball 335 times for 1,752 yards and 16 touchdowns. He also caught five passes for 89 yards and another score. After finishing in the top three of the Heisman voting his first two years Walker ran away with the award, beating Stanford's John Elway and SMU's Eric Dickerson to claim the prize. Georgia finished the regular season with a perfect 11-0 mark and a third straight trip to the Sugar Bowl. They were the top-ranked team in the nation heading into a showdown with second-ranked Penn State. For the second consecutive year, Georgia was denied in the Sugar Bowl, as Penn State was victorious by a 27-23 score.

Walker turned professional following his junior season, but he didn't end up in the NFL. Instead, he signed a deal with the New Jersey Generals of the upstart United States Football League (USFL). The NFL had a rule in place that underclassmen were ineligible to play in the league at that time, so Walker chose to go to the USFL to start his pro career. Walker ran for over 5,500 yards with the Generals in his three years with the team, including a pro football record 2,411-yard season in 1985. The USFL folded after the 1985 season due to financial constraints and a failed antitrust lawsuit against the NFL, which made Walker eligible for the NFL Draft. He was selected by the Dallas Cowboys in the fifth round of the 1985 NFL Draft. He split time with Tony Dorsett his first two years in the league before taking over the starting role in 1988.

Walker was involved in arguably the largest trade in the history of the NFL, and the deal that laid the foundation for the Cowboys dynasty of the early to mid-1990s. He was traded in 1989 to the Minnesota Vikings for five players and six draft choices. The Cowboys parlayed some of those draft choices into the NFL's leading rusher Emmitt Smith, defensive tackle Russell Maryland, cornerback Kevin Smith and safety Darren Woodson. Walker would play for the Cowboys, Vikings, Eagles, and Giants, and he finished his career with a second stint in Dallas before retiring after the 1997 season. Walker was inducted into the College Football Hall of Fame in 1999.

Herschel Walker (#34) carries the ball against the New Orleans Saints during an NFL football game September 20, 1992 at Veterans Stadium in Philadelphia, Pennsylvania. Walker played for the Eagles from 1992-94.

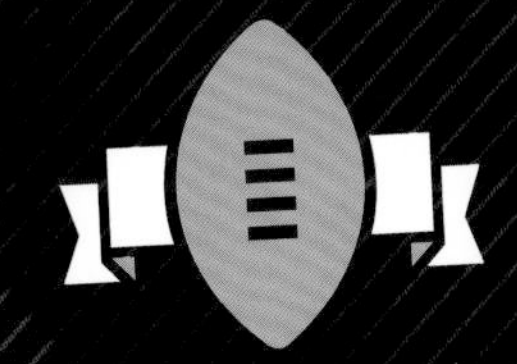

COLLEGE FOOTBALL

MEMORABLE MOMENTS

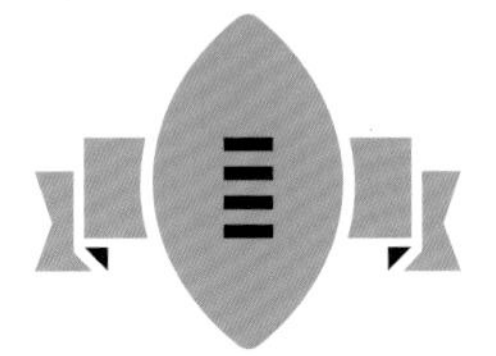

CLASH OF THE TITANS

NOVEMBER 9, 1946
#2 NOTRE DAME FIGHTING IRISH VS
#1 ARMY CADETS

When it comes to epic clashes between top teams in college football, one may be hard pressed to come up with a contest that resonated more with the fans of the sport than the one between Notre Dame and Army in 1946. Contrary to the high-scoring shootouts that are more common these days, the Notre Dame vs Army game was the equivalent of a bare-knuckle brawl that went the distance. Both teams had opportunities to go for a knockout blow after they had staggered their opponent, only to be repulsed by a counterattack.

There was plenty of history between the two schools to add fuel to the fire. In the first half of the twentieth century, Army and its service academy brethren Navy and Air Force were football powerhouses capable of contending for the national championship on a regular basis. Games against highly-touted opponents were normally played on neutral sites to accommodate a larger crowd than could be seated otherwise. Notre Dame drew well, regardless of where the game was played, which added to ticket sales.

As for previous clashes between the two teams, several are memorable. The 1924 tilt between the schools that was held at the Polo Grounds in New York City is one of them. Notre Dame was victorious by a count of 13-7 in an upset victory, and famed sportswriter Grantland Rice dubbed Notre Dame's backfield "The Four Horsemen." Rice coined the nickname after quarterback Harry Stuhldreher, halfbacks Jim Crowley and Don Miller, and fullback Elmer Layden saw the Irish backs run through the vaunted Army defense that day.

There also was the 1928 contest, when, with Notre Dame locked in a scoreless tie with Army at the half, coach Knute Rockne invoked his famous "Win one for the Gipper" speech. George Gipp died in 1920 less than three weeks after his final game at Notre Dame as the result of pneumonia and implored Rockne to tell the team to win one for him one day when the proverbial chips were down. Notre Dame rallied for a pair of touchdowns in the second half and won the game 12-6, further cementing the legacy of Gipp. Army drove to the 1-foot line of Notre Dame in the closing seconds, but time expired before they were able to snap the ball.

In 1946 both teams were undefeated entering the game. Army was the #1 team in the nation, while Notre Dame was ranked second in the country. Army was on a 25-game winning streak; their last defeat was in 1943 by a count of 26-0, fittingly at the hands of Notre Dame. Army had thrashed Notre Dame in 1944 and 1945 by counts of

59-0 and 48-0 respectively, leaving the Irish licking their chops for another shot at redemption against the Cadets.

The game was held at Yankee Stadium, and anticipation was high for the contest. Tickets that sold for US$3.30 in the end zone were selling for $200 on game day. The announced crowd was 74,121, a capacity crowd. Had there been more seats, there was little doubt those would have been sold as well. In fact, Notre Dame had to pay out $500,000 in ticket refunds to people who tried to get seats and were unable to. Things were at a fever pitch to watch the two rivals and the top two teams in the land do battle to determine who the best in the nation was.

In a game that was just as much a chess match between two terrific tactical coaches in Frank Leahy of Notre Dame and Red Blaik of Army as it was the players on the field, the two teams were wary of each other's capabilities and cautious on offense. The end result was very few big plays and a lot of grinding between the tackles. This game is also the only time in college football history that four past or future Heisman Trophy winners shared the field in the same contest. Army's Doc Blanchard (Mr. Inside) won the award in 1945, while Glenn Davis (Mr. Outside) would win it in 1946. Quarterback Johnny Lujack of Notre Dame would claim the coveted statue in 1947, and end Leon Hart would win the award in 1949.

Both teams entered the contest scoring better than 30 points a game. Army was outscoring their opponents by a count of 208-55 coming in, while Notre Dame h[illegible] blitzed their opponents to a tune of 177-18. Neither team boasted a field goal [illegible] Notre Dame's Fred Early didn't even suit up. Lujack has been quoted as [illegible] the Notre Dame coaches had to believe they could score. Another [illegible] coach Leahy didn't believe in field goals, and that "if you couldn't [illegible] taking three points would be an insult. He thought Notre Da[illegible]

View of the action duri[illegible]
the Notre Dame [illegible]

Notre Dame's famous Four Horsemen (L-R): Don Miller (RH), Elmer Hayden (FB), Jim Crowley (LH), and Harry Stuhldreher (QB).

Blanchard was quoted as saying that he couldn't recall ever kicking a field goal. (Jack Ray was actually 1 of 2 kicking field goals in 1946.)

As it turned out, a field goal could have been the decisive strike in the contest, which was ruled by stout defensive performances on both sides of the ball. Despite repeated penetrations into Notre Dame territory in the contest, Army was unable to put any points on the board. Six times Army drove inside the Notre Dame 33-yard line, and each time they were repulsed from putting points up. Lujack made a touchdown-saving tackle on Blanchard in the third quarter. Blanchard's 22-yard run moved the ball to the Notre Dame 36 when Lujack managed to take him down. Blanchard was quoted as saying that he told Lujack if he hadn't injured a knee earlier in the season, he would have ran him over.

Army would drive to the Notre Dame 15-yard line, but the team was thwarted again. Arnold Tucker went back to throw and was intercepted by Irish defensive back and future coach Terry Brennan at the 5-yard line. He would return it 3 yards to the eight, and the threat was quashed. Army would get no closer than that in the entire contest. Tucker had the longest run of the day for Army, a 30-yard scamper that put the ball on the Notre Dame 30 during another drive that came up empty.

Notre Dame had only two drives of note during the contest. One drive stalled at the Army 32, while the other was admittedly the best scoring opportunity of the game for either side. Helped along the way by a 25-yard completion from Lujack to Bob Skoglund, which was the Irish's longest pass of the day, Notre Dame moved inside the Army 10-yard line. Facing third down from the Army 4-yard line, Lujack ran a quarterback sneak and gained a yard to the three. Eschewing the field goal attempt (remember, Early was not even in pads for the game), the Irish opted to go for it. Lujack pitched the ball out on an option run to Bill Gompers to the outside. Gompers was hemmed in and prevented from turning the corner by none other than Davis, who held him up. Hank Foldberg came in to help and knocked Gompers out of bounds for no gain. There was a penalty flag on the play, but it was against Notre Dame for clipping Davis. Army declined the penalty and took the ball over on downs. Just like that, the best Notre Dame drive of the day was finished with nothing to show for it.

Army would cross midfield again in the fourth quarter but had that drive end with a Lujack interception of Tucker in Notre Dame territory. When the final gun sounded, the two teams had battled tooth and nail for 60 minutes and were unable to resolve the conflict with a winner. For that matter, the two sides were unable to put a single point on the board, as defenses ruled the day in a 0-0 deadlock. Both Leahy and Blaik praised the defenses, calling the contest "a terrific battle of defenses." The statistics bear out how much of a defensive struggle the game was.

Lujack completed just 5 of 17 throws in the game for Notre Dame and threw four interceptions. Tucker had three of the interceptions of Lujack in the contest, but threw a pair of his own. Notre Dame also lost three fumbles, while Army lost two. The top two teams in the nation turned the ball over 11 times in a war between the defenses. Notre Dame rung up just 10 first downs, but that was still one more than Army in the game. Notre Dame outrushed Army 173-139 and held the vaunted duo of Davis and Blanchard to just 79 yards in the game. It was the only time in the duo's career that they were held to under 100 combined rushing yards.

The end result of the game led to no change in the polls: Army remained the top team in the land, while Notre Dame stayed #2. Notre Dame would end up being crowned the AP national champion, and Army would carry on their unbeaten streak into 1947 until Columbia snapped it with a 21-20 victory on October 25, 1947.

Halfbacks Glenn D

A TIE FOR THE AGES

NOVEMBER 19, 1966
NOTRE DAME FIGHTING IRISH VS
MICHIGAN STATE SPARTANS

The overblown hyperbole of "Game of the Century" is something that both sports fans and journalists have had to contend with over the past few decades. It seems that every few years, a game that features two highly-ranked teams gets billed as the latest version of the "Game of the Century." A prime example of this was the 2011 regular season clash between the LSU Tigers and the Alabama Crimson Tide. LSU won that game—which may have set college football back a few decades with its ineffective and, in some cases, incompetent offensive showings—9-6 in overtime.

The game between top-ranked Notre Dame and second-ranked Michigan State that took place at Spartan Stadium in East Lansing, Michigan, on November 19, 1966, was tinged with controversy of its own. Before the current rules that instituted overtime, games that were tied at the end of regulation stayed that way. The result of 60 minutes of battle between the Fighting Irish and the Spartans left neither side victorious. The way it ended is still talked about to this day, some 45 years later.

The contest was not nationally televised by ABC, as rules back in 1966 allowed teams one appearance on national television and two appearances in regional broadcasts. Notre Dame had utilized their national appearance in their season-opening 26-14 victory over Purdue, while Michigan State had yet to use theirs. The game was shown on tape delay around the country after an outpouring of letters to ABC headquarters from passionate fans who wanted to see the contest.

Notre Dame entered the game against Michigan State with an 8-0 mark, while the Spartans sported a 9-0 record. It should be noted that going into battle on that frigid day, the Irish were first in the Associated Press poll and second in the UPI, or coaches' poll. Michigan State, meanwhile, was second in the AP poll and first in the coaches' poll. The temperature would not rise above freezing that Saturday, and Notre Dame was dealing with issues before the game ever got started.

Starting running back Nick Eddy, who led Notre Dame in 1966 with 553 yards rushing and 10 touchdowns, did not play a snap in the game. He injured his shoulder hen he slipped on ice while disembarking from the train in East Lansing. That turned ning game duties over to fullback Larry Conjar and backup running back Rocky s didn't get a whole lot better for the Irish in the early going of the game t either. This contest marked the last time that Notre Dame traveled

er around a coach on the
g Irish, East Lansing,

65
60
82
19

Starting quarterback Terry Hanratty, who would finish in the top 10 of the Heisman Trophy voting in 1966, 1967, and 1968, was knocked out of the game in the first quarter with a separated shoulder. Hanratty had scrambled for a 4-yard gain before getting brought down by George Webster. Future NFL Hall of Famer and All-American defensive end Bubba Smith landed on top of Hanratty, flattening him into the turf and doing the damage. He was done for the day, turning the reins of the Irish offense to backup quarterback Coley O'Brien, who was a diabetic. The Irish would also lose starting center George Goedeker to an ankle injury after Notre Dame's first series of the game. The injury happened on Notre Dame's first punt of the day, and he did not return to action.

The teams played a scoreless first quarter, though Michigan State was on the move as the quarter expired. Quarterback Jimmy Raye connected with speedy receiver Gene Washington on a big 42-yard pass play to jump start the Spartans' offense. Michigan State then proceeded to hammer away at Notre Dame with the run. Nine straight running plays later, the Spartans found the end zone. The drive ended when backup fullback Regis Cavender, who was filling in for the injured Bob Apisa, scored from 4 yards out for the first score of the game. Barefoot kicker Dick Kenney booted the extra point, and with 13:20 to play in the opening half, Michigan State took a 7-0 lead over Notre Dame.

The Spartans upped their lead to 10-0 with six minutes to go in the half on Kenney's 47-yard field goal and the announced crowd of 80,011 was deafening. It was the largest crowd in Michigan State history until the two teams battled in 1990 before a

Jimmy Raye (#16) of the Michigan State Spartans hands off to Dwight Lee (#34) as Pete Duranko (#64) of the Notre Dame Fighting Irish pursues.

crowd of 80,401. The field goal was set up by a 30-yard scramble by Raye, who rushed for 75 yards on 21 carries in the contest. Raye would complete just 7 of 22 passes for 142 yards with three interceptions.

The crowd would be quieted though, as just 90 seconds later O'Brien lofted a 34-yard touchdown pass to backup running back Bob Gladieux to cut the lead to 10-7 with 4:30 to go before halftime. Michigan State safety Jess Phillips had a shot at breaking up the pass, but it sailed just out of his reach and into Gladieux's, his only receiving score of the year. The half ended with Michigan State still in front by a count of 10-7. Gladieux would sustain an injury later in the contest and would not return. He also missed the season finale against USC the following week.

The two teams played a scoreless third quarter, with Notre Dame catching a break on a play. Bubba Smith was flagged for being offside, which negated a fumble recovery by the Spartans and left the ball in possession of Notre Dame. Keeping possession on that play proved to be a key event in the contest. Notre Dame still had the ball as the third quarter came to a close, with Michigan State still leading by a field goal, 10-7.

On the opening play of the fourth quarter, Notre Dame's Joe Azzaro kicked a 28-yard field goal. With 14:55 to play in the contest, the game was now tied at 10. Disaster struck Michigan State on the ensuing possession when Raye was intercepted by Tom Schoen for the second time in the contest. Schoen returned the interception to the Michigan State 18-yard line, setting Notre Dame up with excellent field position and a chance to take the lead.

Michigan State defensive end Phil Hoag came up with a huge play, knifing through Notre Dame's blocking scheme to throw running back Dave Haley for an 8-yard loss. Instead of being inside the 20-yard line with a relatively easy field goal, Notre Dame had to attempt a 41-yard kick. Azzaro missed to the right by a small margin; it wo
be the only field goal attempt he would miss all season (he was 4 of 5). Had H
tackled Haley for the loss, Azzaro's kick more than likely would have been

Rear view of Notre D

The two sides exchanged punts for the remainder of the contest. Notre Dame took over with the ball at their 30-yard line with 1:15 to play in the contest. This is where things became extremely controversial. Needing 40 yards or so to get into range for a potential game-winning field goal, Notre Dame coach Ara Parseghian went conservative. With Michigan State in a prevent-style defense to take away the long pass, Parseghian went the other way, running the ball six consecutive times.

Michigan State used their timeouts to preserve time in case Notre Dame was unable to move the chains and get a first down. Facing fourth down, Parseghian took a gamble with the game still very much hanging in the balance and left his offense on the field. They converted the fourth down to keep possession of the ball. O'Brien was sacked on the first down play, then ran for 5 yards on a quarterback keeper as time expired,

(Left to right) Tom O'Leary, Tom Regner, T. Alexander, and Pete Duranko of the Notre Dame Fighting Irish stand on the sidelines before their game against the Michigan State Spartans.

leaving the game a 10-10 tie.

Parseghian was roundly criticized in the press for his conservative play-calling in the final minute. Many pundits felt that Notre Dame should have taken a stab at moving the ball down field in an effort to get into position for a game-winning score. Parseghian was quoted in *Sports Illustrated* as saying: "We'd fought hard to come back and tie it up. After all that, I didn't want to risk giving it to them cheap. They get reckless and it could cost them the game. I wasn't going to do a [...] thing like that at this point."

The Irish were led by O'Brien, who completed 7 of 19 throws for 102 yards and the touchdown pass to Gladieux. He did misfire on his final six passes which, coupled with the prevent defense Michigan State was in, may have swayed Parseghian's way of thinking. Rocky Bleier led Notre Dame with 57 yards on the ground and added three receptions for 16 yards filling in for the injured Eddy. Neither team played in a bowl game in 1966. Notre Dame didn't play in bowls until 1969 as the school felt it would interfere with studies, while Michigan State was hamstrung by rules within the Big Ten Conference. At the time, rules forbid the same school representing the conference in the Rose Bowl in consecutive years. The conference also did not allow teams to play in any bowl but the Rose Bowl.

The star power on the field that crisp November Saturday was mind boggling: 25 of the 44 starters in the game were All-Americans. Michigan State would go on to have four of the top eight picks in the 1967 NFL Draft. Smith went first overall to the Baltimore Colts, running back Clinton Jones was selected second overall by the Minnesota Vikings, Webster went fifth overall to the Houston Oilers, and Washington was the eighth overall pick, also by the Vikings. Not to be outdone, Notre Dame had three first-round selections in the draft as well. Guard Paul Selier was taken by the Jets with the 12th overall pick, defensive end Alan Page was taken 15th overall by Minnesota, and guard Tom Regner was selected 23rd overall by Houston. Page would go on to be enshrined in the Pro Football Hall of Fame.

The conservative play-calling and subsequent tie worked in Notre Dame's favor as the polls kept Notre Dame #1 and Michigan State #2. Notre Dame would go to USC and hand the Trojans their worst loss in school history the next week, 51-0. O'Brien completed 21 of 31 passes for 255 yards and three touchdowns to help the Irish finish the season 9-0-1. The Irish claimed the AP and UPI national championships, and Michigan State was crowned the Football Research poll national champion and the Helms Foundation co-champion. Meanwhile Alabama, who won national championshi
in 1964 and 1965, finished third despite going 11-0 and thrashing Nebraska 34
Sugar Bowl.

THE PLAY

NOVEMBER 20, 1982
CALIFORNIA GOLDEN BEARS VS STANFORD CARDINAL

Over the years, college football has seen some flamboyant personalities, some true greats, Heisman winners who would turn out to be busts in the NFL, monumental upsets for the ages, and a slew of reminders that on any given day between those chalked lines of a football field, anything can happen.

The Play is just one of those examples. In what may be the most incredible finish in college football history—right up there with Doug Flutie to Gerard Phelan in the driving rain at the Orange Bowl, giving Boston College a 47-45 win over Bernie Kosar and the Miami Hurricanes in 1984—the California Golden Bears knocked off their bitter rival, the Stanford Cardinal, by a score of 25-20 on November 20, 1982.

Cal and Stanford's rivalry was called "The Big Game" and this was the 85th such contest between the two schools. Cal was playing for pride and to ruin their rival Stanford's hopes for a bowl berth, as the Cardinal were 5-5 but needed the win to get to six in order to become bowl eligible. Representatives from the Hall of Fame Classic were in attendance, ostensibly to invite the Cardinal should they win the contest.

The Cardinal was led by NFL Hall of Famer John Elway at quarterback in his final collegiate appearance. Elway had racked up 9,000-plus yards and 75 touchdown passes at Stanford but had zero bowl appearances. To get his team to one, he had to beat Cal, touted as "the worst 6-4 team ever," at Cal Memorial Stadium.

After a scoreless opening stanza, Cal took a 3-0 lead midway through the second quarter on a 32-yard Joe Cooper field goal. Later in the second quarter, Cal marched 55 yards in just two plays, with Gale Gilbert connecting with Mariet Ford on a 29-yard touchdown pass to give the Golden Bears a 10-0 advantage with 2:42 to play before the half. Cal took that 10-0 advantage to the locker room at halftime. Gilbert was overshadowed by Elway in this game based on profile and perception; he went on to play in the NFL as a backup quarterback for the Buffalo Bills and San Diego Chargers and was a member of five consecutive Super Bowl teams.

In the third quarter, Elway finally got the Cardinal moving offensively, driving Stanford 80 yards in 11 plays covering 4:02 to get the team on the board. Elway connected with Vincent White on a 2-yard scoring pass. After Mark Harmon booted the extra point, Stanford trailed 10-7 with 5:29 to play in the third quarter. After Stanford's defense stopped Cal cold, the Cardinal took over on their 27-yard line and Elway again quickly moved the team down the field. The Cardinal went 73 yards in five plays, with

...(#7) of the Stanford Cardinal throws a pass.

Elway connecting with White on a 43-yard scoring pass. Harmon's extra point gave Stanford a 14-10 lead with 1:42 to play in the quarter. That was the score entering the final 15 minutes of action.

Gilbert moved Cal 62 yards over 11 plays spanning the end of the third quarter and the beginning of the fourth. Cooper's 35-yard field goal with 13:28 to play cut the Golden Bears' deficit to a single point, 14-13. It should be noted that Cooper was only 2 of 4 kicking field goals on the day. He hit from 31 and 35 but missed from 27 in the first quarter and from 33 yards in the third quarter. Stanford went three-and-out on their ensuing possession and punted the ball away; Cal took the ball over at their 41-yard line. Gilbert took Cal 59 yards in just two plays covering one minute, and he hit Wes Howell for a 32-yard touchdown to give Cal the lead. The attempted two-point conversion failed but Cal had a 19-14 advantage with 11:24 to play in the contest.

After the teams traded punts, Stanford took over on their 20-yard line with 7:38 to play. Elway and the Cardinal went 75 yards in nine plays covering 2:06, and Harmon's 22-yard field goal with 5:32 to play cut Cal's lead to 19-17. The Golden Bears went three-and-out on their next possession but came up with a big play defensively as on second-and-8 from the Cal 33, Eddie White forced Elway to fumble. Gary Plummer recovered the ball at the Cal 37 with 2:32 to play. This time, Stanford's defense held up, stopping John Tuggle on third-and-2 from the Cal 45. Mike Ahr punted 55 yards for a touchback, leaving Stanford with just 1:27 to play and the ball 80 yards from the end zone.

Elway's final drive started on the Stanford 20-yard line, and did so in a negative

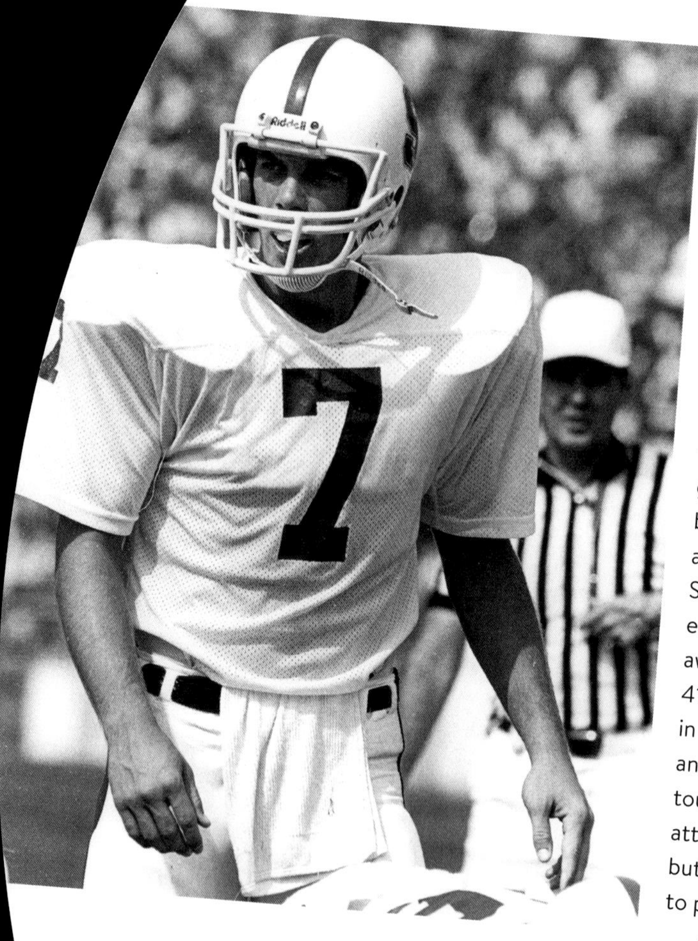

Quarterback John Elway waits to snap the ball.

the ...
for time ...
Harmon ca...
remaining, Stanford ...
getting to a bowl game. ...
meaning they would have to k...
Cardinal were poised to win the Big ...
yards compared to that?

Apparently, it turned out to be everything ... Elway and the Cardinal for their performance and ... Bears now!"

How prophetic that statement was. Harmon squibbed the k... received the ball inside the Cal 45 near the left hash mark. Afte... scrambling, Moen lateraled the ball leftward to Richard Rodgers. Rodg... quickly surrounded, gaining only 1 yard before looking behind him for Dwight ... who caught the ball around the Cal 45. Garner ran straight ahead for 5 yards but w... swallowed up by five Stanford players. While Garner was being tackled, however, he managed to pitch the ball back to Rodgers.

It was at this moment, believing that Garner had been tackled and the game was over, that several Stanford players on the sideline and the entire Stanford band (which had been waiting behind the south end zone) ran onto the field in celebration. TV replays were inconclusive whether Garner was down before he pitched the ball; due to the swarm of tacklers, one cannot see the exact moment his knee touches. Rodgers dodged another Stanford player and took the ball to his right, toward the middle of the field, where at least four other Cal players were ready for the next pitch. Around the Stanford 45, Rodgers pitched the ball to Mariet Ford, who caught it in stride.

Meanwhile, all 144 members of the Stanford band had run out past the south end zone—the one the Cal players were trying to get to—and had advanced as far as 20 yards downfield. The scrum of players was moving towards them. Ford avoided a Stanford player and sprinted up the field while moving to the right of the right hash mark. Around the Stanford 25, three Stanford players smothered Ford, but he threw a blind lateral over his right shoulder. Moen caught it and charged toward the end zone. One Stanford player missed him, and another could not catch him from behind. Moen ran through the scattering Stanford band members for the score, which he famously completed by running into the unaware trombone player Gary Tyrrell, steamrolling him in the process.

The Cal players celebrated wildly, but the officials had not signaled the touchdown. Stanford coach Paul Wiggin and his players argued to the officials that Dwight Garner's knee had been down, rendering what had happened during the rest of the play moot. After a huddle by the officials in which they agreed that none of them had ruled Garner down or blown a whistle, the touchdown was signaled by referee Charles Moffett and a penalty was called on Stanford for illegal participation (for too many Stanford players and the band being on the field), which the officials declined for Cal automatically. The extra point was not even attempted as there was no need; Cal had taken the lead and the game by a 25-20 score.

Referee Charles Moffett had this to say after the contest:

"I called all the officials together and there were some pale faces. The penalty flags were against Stanford for coming onto the field. I say, 'did anybody blow a whistle?' They say 'no.' I say, 'were all the laterals legal'? 'Yes.' Then the line judge, Gordon Riese, says to me, 'Charlie, the guy scored on that.' And I said, 'What?' I had no idea the guy had scored. Actually when I heard that I was kind of relieved. I thought we really would have had a problem if they hadn't scored, because, by the rules, we could have awarded a touchdown [to Cal] for [Stanford] players coming onto the field. I didn't want to have to make that call. I wasn't nervous at all when I stepped out to make the call; maybe I was too dumb. Gee, it seems like it was yesterday. Anyway, when I stepped out of the crowd, there was dead silence in the place. Then when I raised my arms, I thought I had started World War III. It was like an atomic bomb had gone off."

Stanford calls The Play the "Screw of '82" and when they are in possession of the Stanford Axe, they alter the score of the game to read 'Stanford 20-19' instead of the recognized Cal 25-20 victory.

Elway was extremely bitter following the conclusion of the game. He stated:

"I don't think that a touchdown can be scored when you've got a whole band on the field. Now if he runs through three trombone guys, a tuba player, and two drum players, and dodges ... and then runs right over a trombone player at the goal line and they call it a touchdown then, yeah, I think that that probably shouldn't have been called.

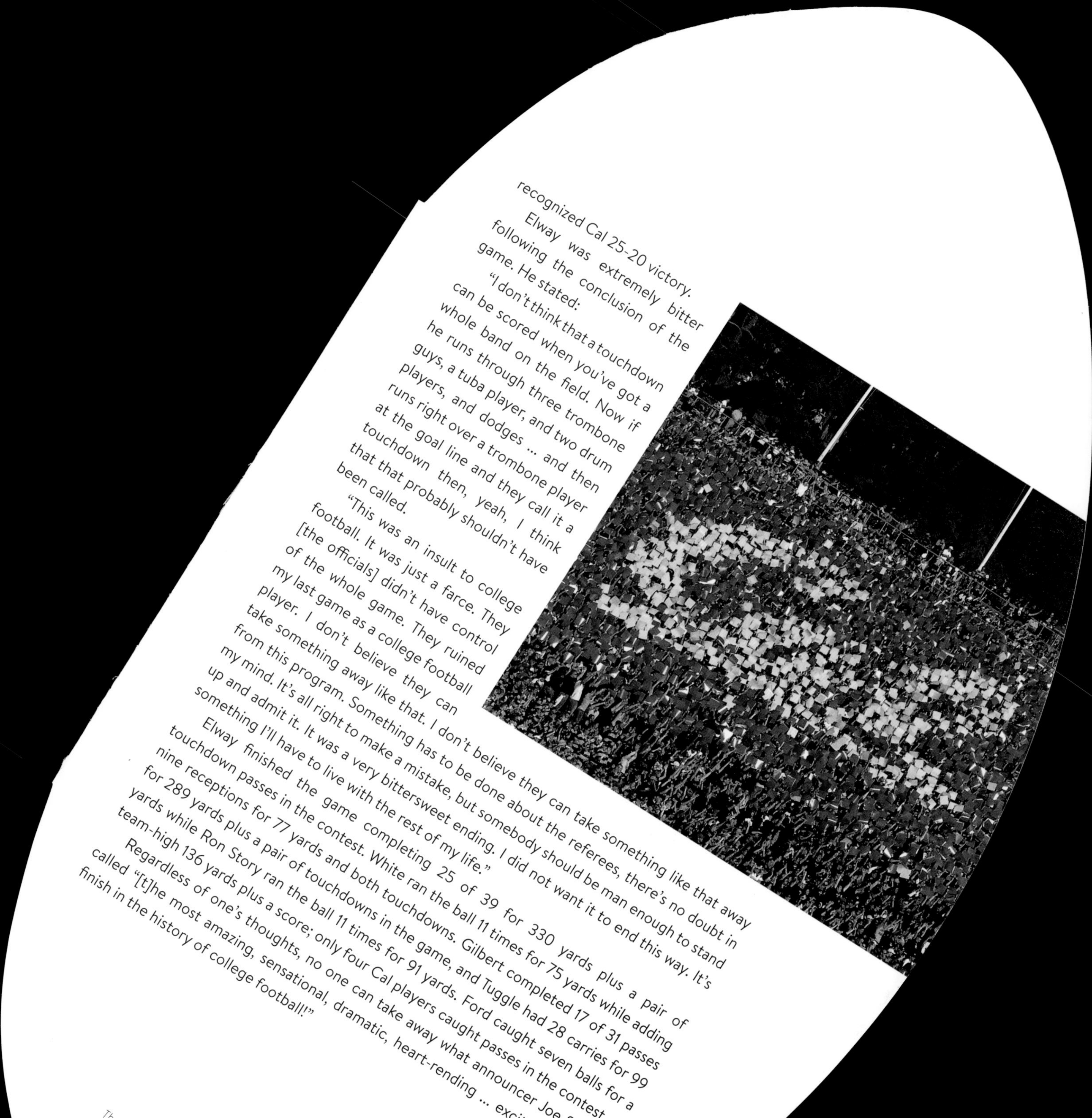

"This was an insult to college football. It was just a farce. They [the officials] didn't have control of the whole game. They ruined my last game as a college football player. I don't believe they can take something away like that. I don't believe they can take something like that away from this program. Something has to be done about the referees, there's no doubt in my mind. It's all right to make a mistake, but somebody should be man enough to stand up and admit it. It was a very bittersweet ending. I did not want it to end this way. It's something I'll have to live with the rest of my life."

Elway finished the game completing 25 of 39 for 330 yards plus a pair of touchdown passes in the contest. White ran the ball 11 times for 75 yards while adding nine receptions for 77 yards and both touchdowns. Gilbert completed 17 of 31 passes for 289 yards plus a pair of touchdowns in the game, and Tuggle had 28 carries for 99 yards while Ron Story ran the ball 11 times for 91 yards. Ford caught seven balls for a team-high 136 yards plus a score; only four Cal players caught passes in the contest.

Regardless of one's thoughts, no one can take away what announcer Joe S... called "[t]he most amazing, sensational, dramatic, heart-rending ... exci... finish in the history of college football!"

IE TO PHELAN

NOVEMBER 23, 1984
BOSTON COLLEGE VS MIAMI (FL)

The date November 23, 1984, may be one that is imprinted on the minds and memories of college football fans around the world. It was the day after Thanksgiving in the United States, a day now commonly known as Black Friday, the start of the Christmas shopping season. There always was football on television that day, and 1984 was no exception. CBS Sports made the decision to move the game between Boston College and Miami from September to November in order to put it in front of a national audience.

Rutgers was originally slated to play Miami that day but agreed to cancel the date with the Hurricanes for a fee of $80,000. The fee was paid by the network executives at CBS, and the game they wanted was secured. It was a clash of two hot prospect quarterbacks: Bernie Kosar at Miami, who had taken over for Jim Kelly after he was drafted in the 1983 NFL Draft, and Doug Flutie at Boston College, a scrambler who maximized his talent and abilities to help Boston College win games.

The Hurricanes were the defending national champions, but entered the game with a record of 8-3 and a #12 ranking in the country. In Miami's previous game, 13 days prior against Maryland, the Hurricanes blew a 31-0 halftime lead as Frank Reich would lead Maryland to a stunning 42-40 come-from-behind victory that was the greatest comeback in college football history at the time. Reich had a penchant for comebacks, and he led the Buffalo Bills to the greatest one in NFL history, rallying Buffalo past Houston 41-38 in overtime of an AFC wild-card playoff game on January 3, 1993. Buffalo trailed 35-3 early in the third quarter of that game after Bubba McDowell intercepted a Reich pass and returned it for a score.

Boston College entered the game ranked 10th in the country with a record of 7-2. They were winners of their previous two games, defeating Syracuse and Army after a tough 37-30 loss to Penn State on November 3. Coach Jack Bicknell and Flutie and company would get a chance to show their abilities in front of a national television audience. The Hurricanes, led by Kosar and first-year coach Jimmy Johnson, would be looking for redemption after the implosion against Maryland.

As the game unfolded, it seemed like Boston College would run away with it early. Boston College scored a pair of touchdowns in the opening nine minutes of play and held a 14-0 lead as the first quarter came to a close. Undaunted, Kosar got the Hurricanes moving in the second quarter, helping Miami knot the game at 14. Flutie would put

Doug Flutie (#22) of the Boston College Eagles congratulates his teammate after a play against the University of Miami Hurricanes at the Orange Bowl

Boston College back up 21-14 on a 9-yard scoring run, and again Kosar answered with a touchdown. He hit Warren Williams in the back of the end zone for an 8-yard scoring pass to tie the game at 21. That would be Williams' lone touchdown reception of the year for Miami. Boston College would strike back on a Flutie-led drive before halftime to give the Eagles a 28-21 advantage at intermission.

Then the rains came. More specifically, it was a deluge as monsoon-type rains bombarded the Orange Bowl and the surrounding area with reckless abandon. When the second half began, the Hurricanes were backed up to their own 4-yard line. It turned out that neither the inclement weather, nor the Boston College defense was capable of stopping the Hurricanes. Kosar led Miami down the field, covering 96 yards and punching it into the end zone to knot the game at 28 apiece. Both teams would kick field goals in the third quarter as well, sending the game to the fourth quarter tied at 31. Those final 15 minutes would be some of the most exciting in the history of college football.

Boston College opened the scoring in the fourth quarter with a field goal to go in front 34-31. Miami struck back with a 52-yard touchdown run by Melvin Bratton to give Miami their first lead of the game at 38-34. Back again came Flutie and Boston College, scoring with 3:50 to play to cap an 82-yard drive and the Eagles led by a 41-38 score.

Doug Flutie congratulates his teammate after a play against the University of Miami Hurricanes at the Orange Bowl.

Stephen Strachan, who would lead Boston College with nine rushing touchdowns in 1984, did the honors from 4 yards out. In a game where the offenses were clicking and the defenses couldn't make a stop, that was an eternity. But the fireworks weren't over yet by any stretch of the imagination.

Boston College seemed to have Miami in a vulnerable spot facing a third down and 21 from their own 10-yard line with 2:30 to play. Instead, Kosar, not known for his maneuverability in the pocket, eluded the Boston College pass rush and evaded being sacked not once, but twice. He eventually fired a completion to Darryl Oliver and managed to move the chains for a first down. Later in the drive, Miami converted a fourth down and one to keep the ball moving.

Miami continued to work the ball downfield, reaching the Boston College 1-yard line inside the final minute of play. Miami called timeout with 30 seconds to go and when play resumed, Bratton went in from a yard out. The extra point gave Miami a 45-41 lead with just 28 seconds left on the clock, and it seemed like Kosar would fire the final shot in what had been a stalwart contest between two field generals.

Boston College, trailing by four with just 28 seconds to play, needed a miracle at this point. The kickoff was a touchback, giving Boston College the ball at their own 20-yard line with no time elapsed. Flutie told his team in the huddle that the plan was to get the ball to midfield and go from there. The Eagles went right to work. Flutie hit running back Troy Stradford out of the backfield for 19 yards up to the Eagle 39-yard line. On the next play, Flutie connected with tight end Scott Gieselman for 13 more yards. Gieselman went out of bounds to stop the clock, with Boston College holding the ball on the Miami 48-yard line. An incomplete pass followed, leaving Boston College 48 yards from the end zone with just six seconds to play.

The play call was "55 Flood Tip," which had three Boston College receivers split out to the right side of the formation. The Eagles practiced the play every week but had only run it three times in the 1984 season. The play worked once, when Gerard Phalen caught a touchdown right before halftime of the Eagles' 24-10 victory over Temple. Kelvin Martin and Stradford stopped near the 5-yard line, while Phalen continued toward the end zone. With the rain and wind, Miami's defensive backs played a step or two closer to the line of scrimmage, thinking Flutie wouldn't be able to get the ball that far in the weather. It was a fatal mistake in a game where the team that had the ball last, regardless of how much time they had, would win the game.

Flutie was flushed from the pocket and had to elude the runaway frei
that was Willie Lee Broughton. Flutie also evaded All-American defensi
Brown, who had a productive NFL career with the Philadelphia Eagl

as he rolled to the right, eventually launching the ball into the air from his own 37-yard line, some 15 yards behind the original line of scrimmage. The ball sailed through the air, farther than the Hurricanes' defensive backs expected. Darrell Fullington and Reggie Sutton both jumped, but the ball floated past their outstretched fingers. All that Miami could do was hope the ball hit the turf, a harmless incompletion that would end the game and preserve their victory. They simply weren't that fortunate.

Phalen, who had gotten behind Fullington and Sutton due to their way of thinking, grabbed the ball just across the goal line and fell into the middle of the end zone, ball in his arms. The official put his arms in the air to signal touchdown. The clock read all zeroes. The sellout crowd at the Orange Bowl was stunned, and Johnson was speechless on the Miami sideline. Bicknell didn't even see the play unfold, as he was knocked down. Flutie was slammed to the turf by Broughton and didn't know what happened until he saw the official signal touchdown. Boston College 47, Miami 45: game over.

It was a fitting ending to a wild shootout between two teams that refused to quit. There were amazing numbers that came out of the game as well. Bernie Kosar completed 25 of 38 throws for 447 yards and two touchdowns. Bratton rushed for 134 yards and added 82 receiving while running for four touchdowns. Oddly, those were the only four rushing touchdowns he had all season long. Eddie Brown, who went over 1,000 yards receiving for Miami in 1984, caught 10 passes for 220 yards for the Hurricanes. Miami totaled 32 first downs and rolled up 655 yards of total offense.

On the other side of the coin, Flutie was 34 of 46 for 472 yards and three touchdowns, while running for a fourth. Phelan caught 11 passes for 226 yards and the game-winning score. Boston College would pick up 30 first downs themselves and total 627 yards of offense. It was the first time in college football history that both quarterbacks threw for more than 300 yards in a game. Boston College would finish the season 10-2 and beat Houston in the Cotton Bowl 45-28. Flutie would win the Heisman Trophy nine days after the game took place, while Kosar finished fourth. Miami lost the Fiesta Bowl to UCLA 39-37, their third loss in a row, all by two points, to finish 8-5.

It was another painful thorn in the side for Fullington. In the game against Maryland, a pass Reich threw deflected off his hands to Terrapin receiver Greg Hill, who went 68 yards for the go-ahead score.

As the saying goes, though, according to former New York Yankees catcher and Baseball Hall of Famer Yogi Berra: "It ain't over til it's over." Those words could not have been more fitting—or prophetic—given the way things unfolded. Twenty-eight seconds was, as it turned out, just long enough for Flutie and the Eagles to steal victory from the jaws of defeat and leave the Hurricanes seeing stars.

Doug Flutie warms up prior to playing.

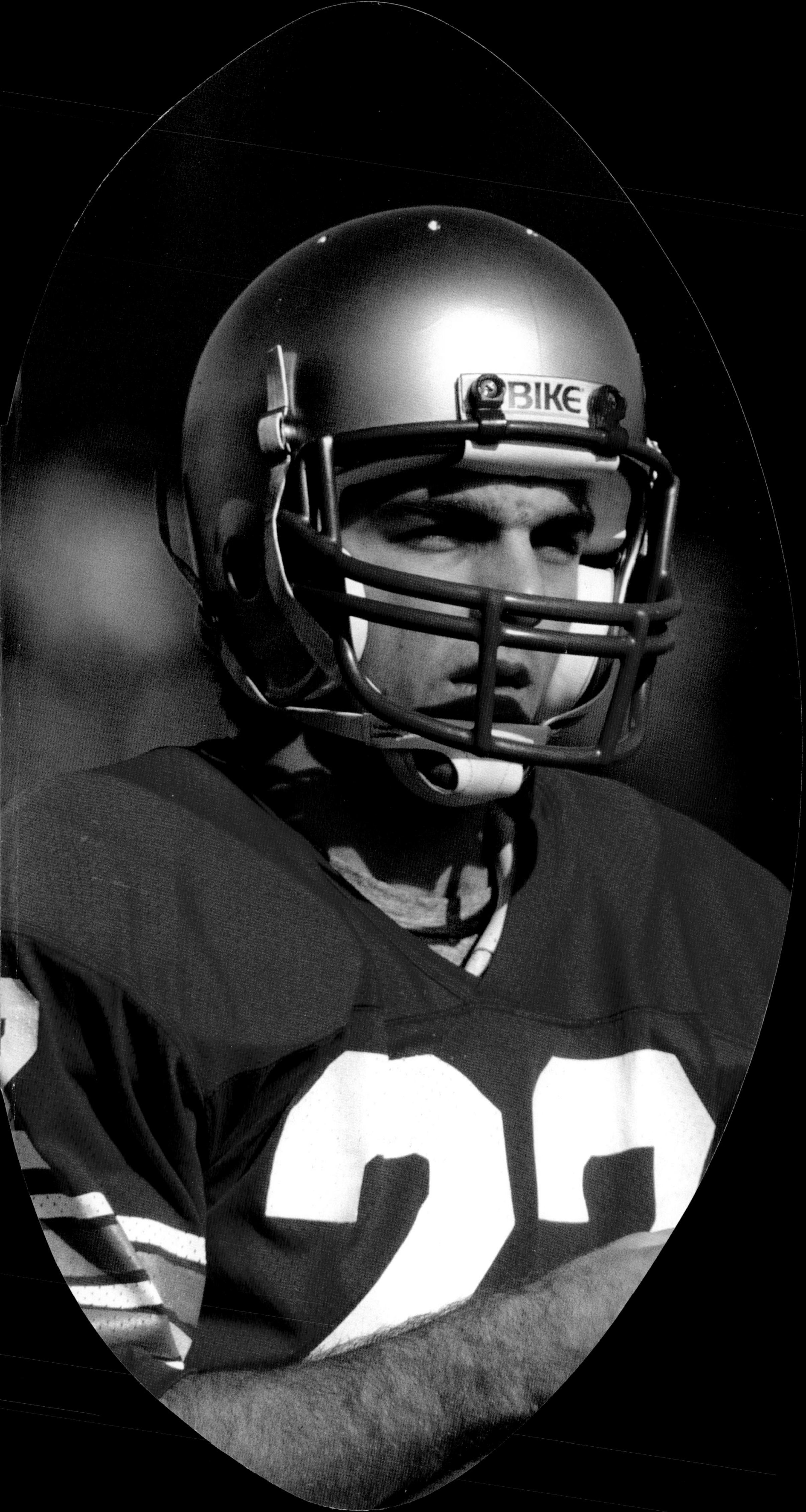
BIKE

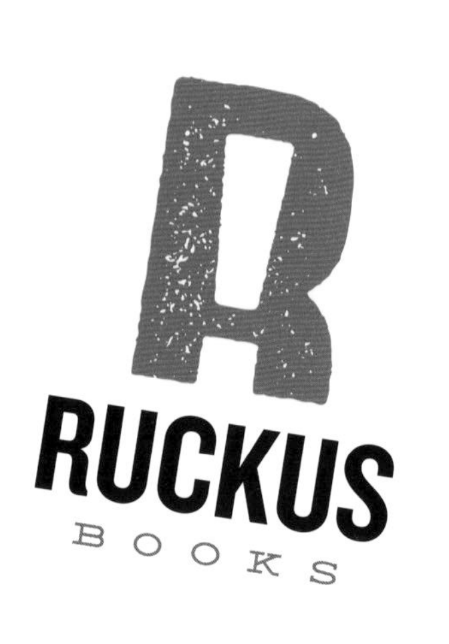
RUCKUS
BOOKS

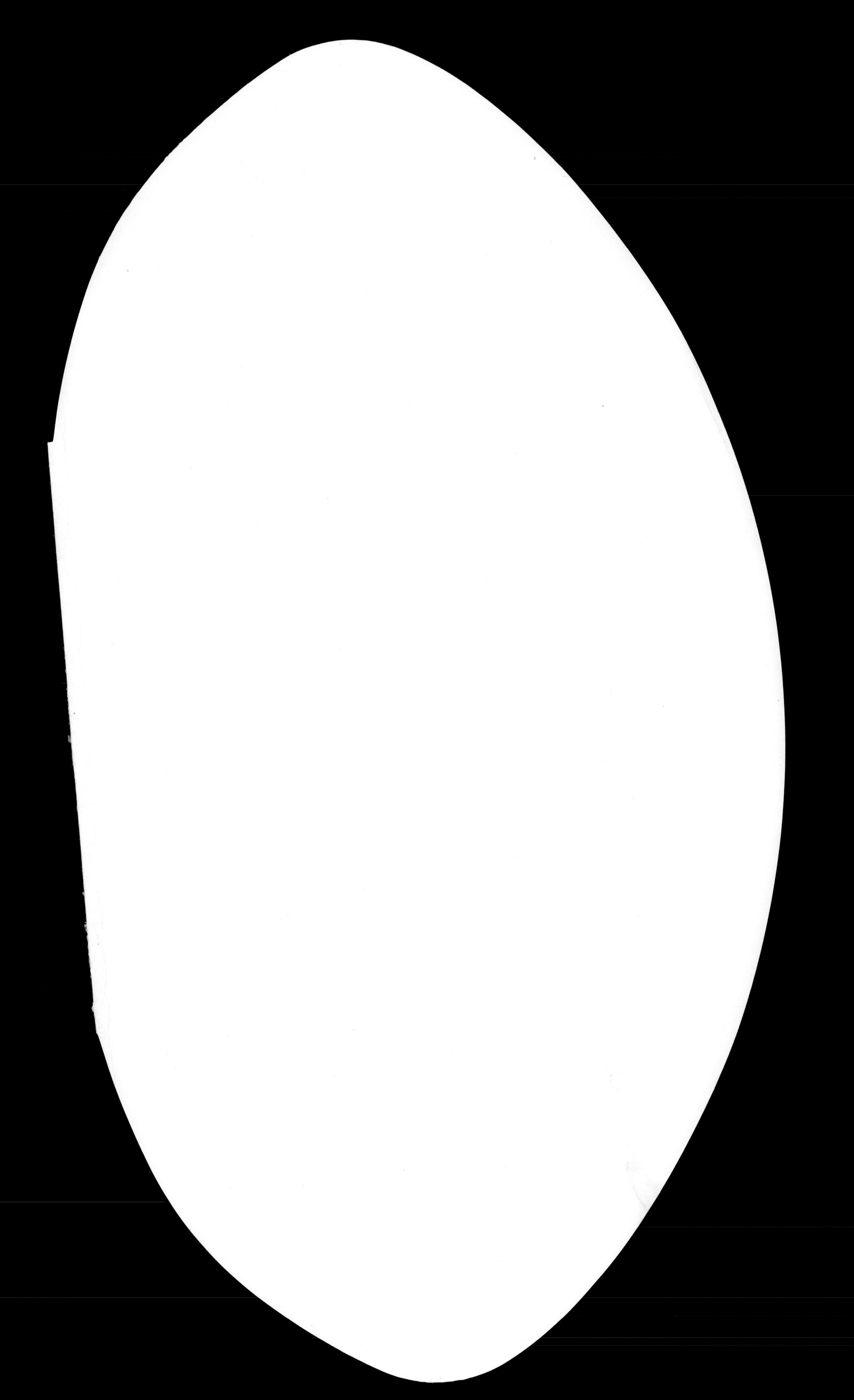

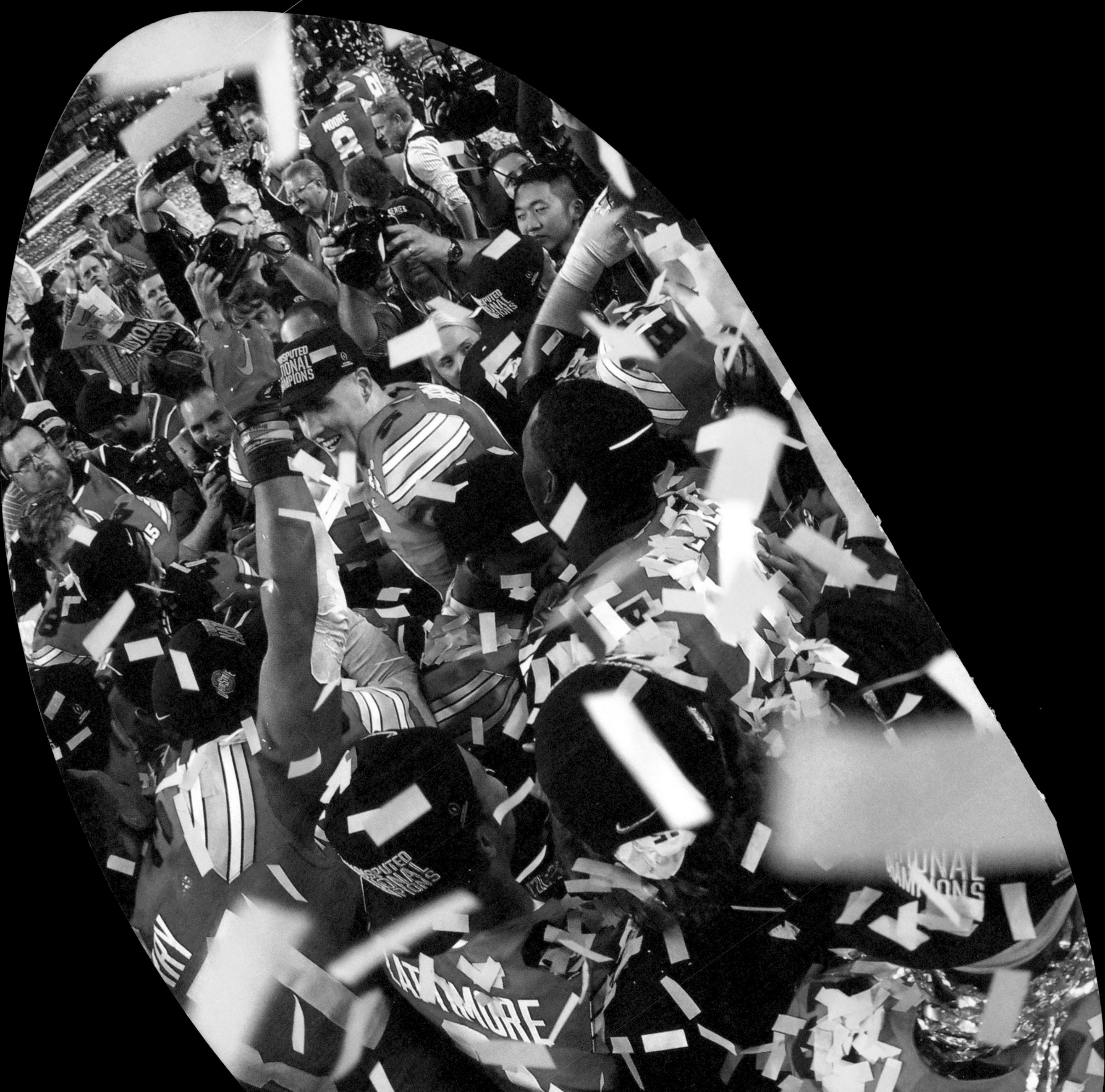
MOORE
CHAMPIONS